Life Co

Complete Blueprint to Becoming a Powerful and Influential Life Coach

Table of Contents

Introduction

I want to thank you and congratulate you for buying the book, "Life Coaching: Complete Blueprint to Becoming a Powerful and Influential Life Coach." Taken from experience of how life coaching works, this book gives you a real blueprint, so that you can base your experience on my experience and that's going to give you a head start. Why? Because you can. Using my vast experience, and not having to go through the same mistakes that I did, means that you are likely to get there faster than the competition.

The most likely reason that you are here is that you think that life coaching is something that you can do or would like to improve upon. Perhaps you want to brush up your skills and become a better life coach than you already are. For those who are not actually aware of what a life coach is, it is a discipline that focuses entirely on what each individual client needs to do and teaches them how to go about it. It also means teaching your clients the importance of setting goals and time limits. That's the short version – as I will give you more details later in the book. Your optimism and enthusiasm are vital to the equation. You must also make your client confident that you know what you're talking about.

The outcome that most people who visit a life coach are looking for is more certainty and confidence. And to help them achieve that, you must find out what they want – never what they don't want. Then you must find out why they want it and what it will give them once they achieve a certain level of competency. Once you have those answers, you can begin your life coaching sessions clearly in the knowledge of what your client needs from you. In fact, each plan that I put forward to a client is specifically designed to suit that client's needs, bearing in mind the initial interview with a proposed client, to establish the aforementioned information. If you know what a client wants, you are half way there. The rest is down to your plan and the execution of that plan. It's not about giving advice. It's about teaching your client another way to look at life's problems and giving them concrete ways in which they can reach their goals.

This book contains very useful information on how to become a true authority in the field of life coaching. You may be reading this book because you have an innate passion for helping other people. That passion can be one of your best assets in becoming an influential life coach. But your passion to help other people is not enough for you to become truly successful. Throughout this book, you will learn the other things that you need to include in order to become a great life coach. Great means getting past mediocre. It means understanding people – what they want and what they are able to achieve with your help. That takes skill. Thanks again for buying this book, I hope that it helps you to find the answers you need and to hone the skills needed to really be successful as a coach. The blueprint will of course differ for each type of life coaching, but the essentials included here will be enough to help you form the basis of what you teach to your students. If you have a positive outlook, you've come to the right place. The blueprints that are included within the book show you what you need to accomplish to set up your business, how to approach potential clients, how to sell yourself and to persuade them to listen and to hire you.

There are some wonderful examples of life coaches out there, but there are also the mediocre coaches who haven't done their homework and whose blueprint isn't the same as that given in this book. Their approach is too random. They perhaps haven't done their homework and wonder why they have such a small client base. Take it from me, if you want a larger client base, you have to lure them in such a way as to make what you have to offer irresistible. Once you do, you will have clients eating off your hands and begging for what you have to offer them.

It's a wonderful opportunity to shine but you can only shine if you are prepared to go through all aspects of the blueprint. People may not know who you are at this moment in time but if you have the makings of a life coach, it won't be long before your target audience is sitting up and taking notice. This book helps you to make your approach in a professional manner and start to use your skills, your education and your entrepreneurial spirit to help others achieve those things they seek to achieve. That's satisfying. That's life changing and it's all down to your approach, your professionalism and your ability to sell yourself without looking cheap.

Life coaching as a profession is suitable for those who have a very positive outlook on life and who are able to work out systems that enable others to gain from the experience of coaching. It is a very different thing to teaching, since you don't teach. You simply show your clients methods whereby they can achieve the results that they want and look at their lives in a different manner, as well as learning techniques that permit them to reach goals much more easily. Often it is the approach that someone makes toward life goals that holds them back because they put too many obstacles in the way of achievement. Life coaching takes those obstacles away and allows the individual to learn how to make themselves free of them so that their future is assured to be set in the right direction for success. That success will be measured differently by different clients and this is all explained within the pages of this book. Life coaching is a complex job but an extremely rewarding one when you know that your job helped someone else to succeed. That buzz you feel from that experience cannot be put into words, but shows in the smiles of clients who achieve what it is that they are aiming at – going forward into their lives with a wealth of new experience and methodology that enriches their lives.

CHAPTER 1

Different Types of Life Coach

Life coaching is something that many people choose to use to improve themselves, to increase their motivation, deal with the problems that life throws at them and learn a few new skills along the way. Life coaches are there to guide them through the issues they face, like a change in career or relationships, health problems or stress. Some life coaches provide a general service while others tend to specialize in a specific area, like health and fitness, mental health, career, financial or even such diverse things as relationships.

It is widely said that a life coach needs no formal education or training but there are those who choose to gain certification from colleges and institutions because these give them more clout against the competition. Being certified tells prospective clients that you have gone through training to do the job and it gives them more confidence in your abilities. However, as it is not a regulated industry anyone can offer training courses or seminars, with some adverts claiming that they can fully train a life coach within 3 hours. I believe that if you have the instinct and character to become a coach, you will be successful at it. You will need that confidence to be able to spread your message. Below is an overview of each of the specialist kinds of life coach:

Career and Financial Life Coaching

Life coaches who choose to specialize in careers and finances will see clients who are struggling in their careers – maybe people who feel that they are going nowhere or are always being passed over for promotion – or those who are making changes to their careers like retiring or seeking a brand new career path.

They will also provide guidance for those who have entered a mid-life crisis, are struggling financially, who needs help with managing money, having budgeting and spending problems. A therapist will look for an underlying mental health issue or perhaps psychological issues that are related to the career or finance issues but a life coach will focus their attention on the problem itself. They will provide the necessary guidance, advice, feedback and helpful blueprint on how their clients can help themselves to achieve their goals. In this day and age, with so much competition out there, it's little wonder that those who are not as successful as they would like to be seek the help of a coach. It can make a whole difference to their career path. It can help clients to understand money management and be able to fulfill things they only dreamed about. A life coach is a little bit of hope in the struggle toward feeling that all important sense of self-achievement that is necessary for the wellbeing of everyone.

Relationship and Family Life Coaches

If you have relationship issues, family problems or dating problems, you might head straight for a traditional therapist who will talk to you, discuss the issues, your feelings and try to determine the underlying issues. They won't actually give you any direct advice although they will give you some tips or feedback relating to your character and the way in which it needs improving. However, you might consider seeing a life coach who specializes in relationships and family issues because this is a different thing altogether to having therapy. In therapy, you are asked to look at things from a mental attitude point of view. However, coaches will provide you with direct advice based on your specific problem and they will also provide a means to help you to improve the way that people see you and your ability to communicate. Life coaches who specialize in these areas focus on the present time, not on the past, and they will guide you towards a solution that will help you to solve the problem you have.

You must bear in mind that therapy may be sought by those who have baggage from the past that they can't let go of. A therapist will analyze it and be able to help strengthen your resistance to problems of this nature. A life coach, on the other hand, will teach you to move forward and show you just how irrelevant past experience is to the "now."

Health and Wellness Life Coaches

A health and wellness life coach specializes in guiding a person who needs help with a weight problem, getting fit, starting an exercise regime, having the right nutrition, dieting problems, stress and other health and medical concerns that may have an effect on their ability to lose or gain weight. A lot of health and wellness life coaches are also fully trained nutritionists and fitness trainers. They will address issues like over or under eating, compulsive dieting, bad eating habits and other issues that are related to these areas of life.

However, if you are suffering from a medical issue or are thoroughly demotivated, life coaching is only part of the equation and you will need to seek medical advice as well. If you are thinking of going in for this type of coaching, then it's best that you do get qualifications before entertaining the idea of helping clients. By getting the appropriate certification, this will also help you to work hand in hand with clinics that can pass patients your way if they believe that your services would be of use to those clients they see regularly who make no improvement on their own.

Health and wellness life coaches are those people who can help motivate clients to making wise decisions and moving on with their lives in a positive way. Because coaches are paid for their services and are extremely respected, it's quite possible that demand in this field will be high, which is another good reason to have nutritional and fitness training qualifications.

Mental Health Life Coaches

Mental health life coaches will not specifically address a psychological or psychiatric problem and should not be seen as the alternative to a professional medical consultation. Mental health life coaches are rarely trained to the degree that is needed to provide guidance on severe depression, stress or anxiety disorders. However, they can help and guide a client who is experiencing grief after the loss of a loved one, anger management issues and conflict resolution. They can also provide guidance in spirituality, confidence and balance or help a client to find their senses of purpose in life. They teach you how to manage stress, anger and improve communication skills, helping their clients to attain their goals.

Many celebrities seek the help of life coaches of this nature because they have problems trying to find answers in life. If you choose to have a career in this field, you would do well to learn about the different aspects of life that can be reinforced to help people to get beyond their initial anxieties in life. As this relates to mental health and wellbeing, you may also need to be in touch with mental health experts in case clients have specific needs that cannot be addressed under the guise of life coach. Often people are not sure of the purpose of their lives and can't see a way ahead. This can happen in the case of celebrities because of the fast lifestyle and life coaches help them to find answers to help them to approach life in a different manner, a manner that gives them more satisfaction, focus and purpose.

That's a lot of territory and you may find that your practice covers overlaps of each kind of coaching, though specializing helps you to get to the top of your field of coaching. Helping people to make the most of their lives is what coaching is all about and it's vital therefore that you are confident, that you know different methods to suit different personalities and that you have a strong enough personality to carry your message to clients. Make no mistake. I have reinforced time and time again during the writing of this book that it's not about giving out advice. It's about teaching people to achieve what they feel they need to achieve using methods that you will learn in your role as a life coach.

In this day and age, life coaching through the Internet is entirely possible, so it's to your advantage to seek out what life coaches are offering through social networking sites such as LinkedIn for business and career coaching, Facebook for lifestyle and relationship coaching and YouTube for all kinds of coaching, so that you can spread your name sufficiently to gain an online presence that people sit up and take notice of. If you have social media such as video presentations, these can be very useful to pinpoint who you are and what you offer to people or businesses. Many life coaches who work in business are actually paid by employers to help staff to gain more enthusiasm and a certain level of achievement and thus, the better your presentation, the more likely you are to be asked to participate and help out with staff training. Life coaching is a very lucrative business to be in and this book provides the blueprints that will help you to succeed.

CHAPTER 2

Life Coaching As a Career

What is a Life Coach?

A life coach is basically someone who works closely with a client on a one-to-one basis in order to assist the client in determining and achieving his or her professional or personal goals. A life coach utilizes a number of different specialized techniques during the entire life coaching process with the aim of supporting the client in setting and achieving their objectives and goals. They may also be asked to cater for groups and this works well too because the teamwork between the speakers and the participants can really help to deal with specific problems which may be universal to people looking for help, especially in a specific group setting.

In the initial days of coaching, only the rich executive types and ambitious career people availed themselves of the services of life coaches. Now, more and more people are becoming aware of the benefits of life coaching and are seeking the expertise of a life coach in attaining their various professional and personal goals. You can see life coaches in all areas of life and if you are thinking of taking this up as a career, you need to know which area you feel you would be particularly suited to.

The work of a life coach consists of three primary tasks. The first task is to closely work with a client in order to aid them in examining their career and life, as a whole, from an objective standpoint. The second task is to help the client determine who they really are, what their true desires are and what they truly want to achieve in life based on the new perspective that they have gained from the first task. The third task is to provide the clients with support and effective tools and techniques in working towards the achievement of those dreams and goals.

A lot of people actually confuse life coaching with therapy or management consulting. What you need to understand is that a life coach is neither a business consultant nor a counselor. This is important for you to grasp and explain to your clients so that you will be able to explain what they can expect from their partnership with you. Employing a life coach, a client needs to understand that the client's participation is vital to their success. Things don't change on their own and a life coach can tell people how to change their approach so that all of those required events happen. They cannot, however, make them happen without the client taking an active part.

A life coach needs to have a set of specialized skills such as goal setting and values assessment that are effective in supporting and training clients to recognize what they truly desire and in helping clients determine the most effective steps that can be taken to achieve those desires.

Many people choose life coaching as a career because of the great flexibility that it provides. As a life coach, you can do your job in just about any location that suits your lifestyle. The only requirement is the relative privacy of the location to ensure that you and your client will not be disturbed during your life coaching sessions. The work hours is also very flexible and it greatly depends on the amount of time that each of your clients require based on their circumstances and goals. If you do choose to life coach online, this time can be flexible and you will be able to have private meetings with a client on the other side of the world if you want to, simply by using the technology available these days – such as Skype and Google Hangouts.

In general, you will be required to meet with each of your clients at preset intervals during the whole coaching period that normally lasts for 3 months. If you are employed, your employer will determine the number of clients that you will handle. But if you are working on your own, the standard is to have at least five clients each week with a maximum of twenty clients each week. You need to bear in mind that you may have to do homework between sessions to cater for individual needs that you have not dealt with before. You also need to give clients quality time, so it is best not to take on more clients than you can handle. You may also need to give additional life coaching sessions to clients, if you deem that they need it. Really, you need to follow your gut instinct. If you work for an established company, then their guidelines come first and you will be expected to work within them, even if your methodology is a little different to that which they are accustomed to. Make allowance too for lectures since these are a great opportunity to spread the word of your services and to share the podium with other like-minded life coaches.

One of the critical things that you need to have as a life coach is your connection with your clients. Generally, life-coaching companies make the effort of ensuring a "good match" between the life coach and the prospective clients. This is critical since life coaching is truly a partnership between the life coach and the client where both of them contribute to the achievement of the client's goals and attainment of the client's dreams in life. If the life coach and the client are not compatible, it is doubtful that they can effectively work together in achieving the partnership's objectives. For this reason, meeting potential clients in a preliminary session is always a good idea.

One of the driving factors in a life-coaching career is your passion for helping other people. But other than that passion, you also need to get enough mentoring or coaching supervision before you can become a successful life coach. And even when you are already well into your life-coaching career, you still need to continuously seek ways to improve your skills and techniques. This will enable you to know how to properly deal with different kinds of emotions and situations that your clients may face. You need to learn how to tackle your clients' problems without making them into your own problems. That takes practice and professionalism.

Life coach training is considered as one of the best ways to prepare for becoming an effective life coach. Through training, you will be able to learn how to deal with different types of issues and the techniques and skills that you need to help your clients become successful. You will learn some of the most effective methodologies used in life coaching such as mentoring, goal setting, values assessment, behavior modeling and behavior modification processes. But you always need to keep in mind that, more than acquiring all these skills and techniques, you should always have the passion for helping other people achieve contentment and happiness not only in their careers but in their lives, in general.

Salary and Employment

Life coaches are typically self-employed but there are some life coaches who choose to become employed by big institutions. According to PayScale.com, the average salary for life coaches is around $29 per hour. The rate that you can get will depend on your experience. But it has also been noted that most life coaches eventually move on to other careers or job positions after twenty years or so of life coaching. That depends upon you. They may also work in groups and develop their life coaching into different areas as their experience evolves. You need to be energetic, dynamic and positive and that can take a toll on you after that much time. In my case, I have been coaching for more than 15 years and don't see any change in that for the rest of my career, other than learning more new methods and being able to help more people look forward to more fulfilling lives.

Becoming a guru is something many people want to do but some will opt for the title of life coach. Everyone wants to earn a small fortune doing a job they think they are good at but, in reality, very few life coaches earn more than $100,000 a year doing their jobs. Not only that, there has been a recent boom in life coaching and clients have a lot of different coaches to choose from. That means your prices have to be competitive if you want to get a foothold in the market. There are three factors that will affect the salary you can earn as a life coach – the area you choose to specialize in, your expertise and qualifications and your client profile. I am going to give you a brief overview of the average salary range on a per-specialty basis, along with an example of a top life-coaching guru for each one.

Life Coaching by Specialty

Because there is a huge variation in what life coaches do, the salary varies across these specialties. Most life coaches will be found in human resources and social services positions. Many human resources departments will have a life coach on board who is responsible for market research and personality tests that are designed to help those searching for a job or with developing their career. A large number of retired athletes and sports trainers go on to become life coaches with their main emphasis being on the health, fitness and nutrition elements while other people go on to work in the business, financial or family life coaching areas. The area I work in is in relationships and that's a very rewarding place for me to be because I understand the dynamics that get in the way of people being able to make and keep friendships, or get over events such as divorce or loss. The dynamics of a family are also very interesting, especially from the perspective of changes that are happening in this day and age where blended families are more common. If you work in this kind of area, it's quite likely that you will settle for a salary that isn't that great but the satisfaction you get from the job more than makes up for it.

Financial Services Coaching

A lot of financial life coaches develop their own coaching services and products and sell them online, alongside financial products and advice. A typical salary for a financial life coach is between $40-60,000 with about one third bringing in $80,000 or above. Financial life coaches not only promise to help you gain financial freedom and wealth now, they also work very closely with their clients to develop their professional and personal goals.

Tony Robbins is a leading life coach in the business arena and, at the tender age of 19, claimed he was earning in excess of $10,000 a month. These days he has much more competition to contend with but is still one of the top earners. Tony Robbins has also developed training for life coaches and it's interesting to note that his business is getting larger as his team expands, offering people a thirty minute interview before actually getting to the nitty gritty of life coaching. I think that's a fairly healthy approach to life coaching because you cannot make two people get on and if a coach proves to be unsuitable to a client, this initial interview helps the client to ensure that the coach chosen is one that they are willing and able to work with. Having a team has many benefits because you can reap business where an individual coach may fail due to conflict of character.

Personal and Professional Development Coaching

Many life coaches in this specialty area are psychiatrists who are employed at institutions. They provide counseling for both life and career issues as part of rehabilitation and recovery programs. Private practice life coaches specialize in a much broader spectrum and may cover both psychotherapy and positive psychology. Those in the middle of their career can earn between $60,000 and $80,000.

Dr. Phil is a psychologist who specializes in this type of life coaching and is one of the leading gurus. His net worth is somewhere in the region of $245 million. Don't expect that straight away but you can learn a great deal by understanding his style and the presence that he has made on the coaching circuit. Watch some of his YouTube videos, and these give you an idea as to why he has become a personality in his own right and is so successful at what he does. Remember as well that this guy has qualifications and didn't get there based on just his personality. If you want the big bucks, then you may have to get the qualifications that actually give you a head start. Then, work on your techniques and practice and become well known for what you offer your clients. Remember one satisfied client is a potential word of mouth recommendation for others. Thus, never dismiss a client's needs. If you get a bad reputation, it works the other way and you may find yourself looking out for another career. In this area, it's essential that you respect the confidentiality of your clients and it certainly won't help your career if you betray it.

Sports, Health, and Fitness Coaches

Sports coaches are very highly paid public employees in the US with a small minority netting $5 million a year. Not many are going to turn their nose up at that kind of money but, once age takes over and their winning streak turns in the opposite direction, many sportsmen turn to private coaching instead, although they won't make anywhere near the money they made as a public sports coach. However, there are areas that you can excel in with the right qualifications. Fitness and

Nutrition are high on the agenda right now with so many people being obese. Would you rather go and queue up in a public practice in full view of others in a situation like this, or do you have the money to pay a private coach? If you do have the money, having a private coach can help you to overcome those health issues that are holding you back. Thus, the first thing to consider with this type of work is qualifications – looking into the market for jobs and establishing yourself. Then, you can expand your business to the Internet and TV area or simply private practice. If you have the money for your own gym, then you can also train your staff to use your methods.

This is a business that you can start near your home and with the right equipment and the right tactical approach, you can set targets for your clients and teach them new ways of thinking in order to achieve their goals. This is a great area for people who are good communicators and who are extremely positive, since many of the clients dealt with will come to you with a negative outlook.

Business Life Coaches

This is the single biggest sector and the fastest growing one in life coaching. Many people yearn to be at the top, with the likes of Tom Peters or Michael Porter but they have a long way to go. A top business life coach will stay up through the night working out how to get the edge on the competition. If you can get yourself to the position of thought leader, your services will definitely be in demand because these are the coaches who win the clients in the biggest and the most successful companies in the world. If you can persuade big companies to employ you as a life coach for their business, you stand to earn good money, but they won't employ you just based upon what you say. They will want to know who you are and what you bring to the table.

Business gurus come and go and small business coaching is not something that should be brushed aside. In fact, there is an extremely high demand for small business life coaches and leadership coaches. The demand mirrors that of business consulting and, with bonuses, a junior consultant will earn around $72,000, a senior around $110,000 while a senior partner can take home $280,000 a year.

Spiritual Life Coach

Income varies quite widely for the spiritual life coach. Most people tend to think of spiritual life coaching as being yoga or meditation and, unlike Western society, an Asian spiritual life coach is less likely to charge for their services or, if they do, it will be the minimum amount required to cover their needs. One of the top spiritual life coaches, Eckhart Tolle, takes in an annual salary of $3.75 million.

Spiritual life coaches are not just gurus. Many teach clients to use different methods to reach their spiritual goals. Yes, there are gurus but this is an area where your expectations should be a little humbler at the beginning until you have a proven track record and recommendations from clients and know what it is that you are offering that other coaches do not. Remember it is not a case of using advice. It's a case of knowing how to direct a client to discover their spiritual capabilities on their own using methods that are tried and tested so you will need to have knowledge. You can't do this, for example, from textbooks. You need to have experienced it and be able to share with your clients how they can experience it too.

The Level of Expertise and Qualifications Needed

If you have the right qualifications, it is very easy to become a professional life coach. As the salaries we mentioned above show, the market would pay for the right experience and the right qualifications if you are able to sell your services. This is one reason why personality is so important to life coaching. Junior partners will always earn less than a senior partner but how much they earn depends entirely on how their advice is valued by the market. Many business consultants have a dream of starting up their own life coaching business one day but kicking it off too early could set you back both financially and career-wise. The safest option is to start building up your life-coaching career slowly, alongside other businesses such as a health and fitness consultation business or another financial advice service. If you want to work in the field of business, then starting with companies who recruit and train employees is the ideal because you will get to gain a reputation which will enable you to branch out on your own once you are established.

Most life-coaching gurus reached the absolute top level in the corporate world before they turned to life coaching as a career. Sports coaches who have coached some of the top teams in the world can command top dollar as a life coach as can a top athlete who has a string of medals. Nikki Stone is a two-time gold medal winner for the US team in aerial skiing and she backed up those medals with a full degree in sports psychology before becoming a successful author and motivational speaker.

Life Coach Salary by Client Profile

A life coach who targets professional athletes or senior business executives can command the highest fees. The trick is to start low and build up your experience in your chosen area before you step into a career as a life coach. The more knowledge and experience you bring to the table, the more choice of clients you will have to pick from. Once your name gets around, you will find that clients come to you because of that reputation that you have gained and you need to keep up to date with techniques and ways to keep your client base motivated.

What are the responsibilities of a Life Coach?

Here are some of the responsibilities that you will undertake if ever you choose to take up the career of a life coach:

- You will work with clients for a typical period of three to six months in order to help them attain their goals. Goals will have to be tailored to the client.

- You can opt to work with your clients on a one on one basis or within a group, depending on the objectives of your clients.

- You are required to practice utmost confidentiality in order to create a trusting and safe relationship for your clients. Remember that their trust in you is paramount to success.

- After you have established a relationship with your clients, you need to promote working in partnership with them. You need to meet at least once a month to discuss the clients' progress or any issues that they may have. Expect meetings to be more regular than this for personal relationship coaches and at the commencement of the coaching experience.

- You should be able to help your clients discover what they truly want to achieve. You need to help your clients create realistic goals for themselves. The goals that your clients will make should be tailored according to their specific needs. Keep an open mind because some clients may have specific goals that they need help with. If these fall outside your level of expertise, you need to be able to deal with the inquiries professionally and be able to refer them to someone more appropriate.

- You need to create a personalized program for each of your clients that will enable them to achieve their goals. You can't do this on a standard basis, but if you are working with a certain company, those goals can be spread among employees who are taking the same course with you.

- You should provide support to your clients in every step of the program. You will also be required to monitor the progress of your clients in achieving their goals so that you can make the necessary adjustments in the program when some of the steps are not working or certain issues arise.

One last thing that I would add is that as a life coach you can expect to work harder than you ever have done in your life. It's a pleasure if you have the right calling and you will find that you automatically work more hours than you should but it's all part and parcel of what's to be expected. Think of it this way – doctors and other caring trades expect trainees to put unreasonable hours into their training and they certainly do. In coaching though, your own enthusiasm will get you up in the middle of the night because you find it hard to keep new ideas to yourself. It's part and parcel of the makeup of your personality.

Client meetings are person-to-person, via the phone or through video chat sessions. They can range from once or twice a week to once a month, depending on the personal situation of the client and what their goals are. Around 31% of life coaches deal with concerns that are business related, like issues with staff and team effectiveness; 36% specialize in relationship issues, especially interpersonal relationships while 31% deal with a range of other issues. After the first client meeting, the issues should have been revealed and a number of solutions discussed. At this point, the life coach draws up the development plan and would discuss specific goals that the client must attain before the next meeting is scheduled. Alternatively, offering a 30 minute session to discuss what you do can be followed up by the client as and when they have decided to commit to your services.

Life coaches are generally skilled at getting their clients to open up about their problems. They are able to get the client to look inside him or herself and determine what the problem is that is holding them back. To some questions that a life coach asks, the client response will be along the lines of "I don't know." A life coach would turn that around and ask the client what the answer to the question would be if the client did know. This is designed to make the client see that he or she really does have all the answers. They just need help putting them into a plan. Another question you might ask your client is "What needs to happen if you are going to achieve this?" This is designed to separate the things that must happen from those that are negotiable in terms of whether they should be done or not. It makes the client see that there are specific steps that they must take if they are to solve the problem. Life coaches are also good at reframing a situation and asking a client to look at the problem from a different perspective. This helps them to determine if there are genuine obstacles or just excuses in the way of the solution.

The job benefits of being a life coach include the ability to be able to work from home, be your own boss and have a flexible working schedule. Many life coaches gain a lot of joy and satisfaction from helping other people to succeed and, as a result of the hard work on both sides, the life coach is able to see the effect of their work in the client's personal, family and working life. They also enjoy tremendously the success of their clients following consultation.

Who are qualified to become a life coach?

Currently, there are no regulations governing the life coaching industry. But for you to become a life coach, you need to have formal qualifications because people will want to see what your qualifications are in order to have confidence in your services. It is ideal that you obtain training from the International Coaching Federation. One of the programs that they offer is the Certificate in Professional Coaching Practice.

If you are going to work in the relationships or grief area of coaching, then working for a charitable organization such as the Samaritans who deal with calls every day from troubled people will help. These give you great insight as to how to deal with people whose problems really are much too big for them to see any logical conclusion. Organizations such as this train all their telephone operators in psychologically, being able to listen without judgment and being able to use mirroring as an effective way to help troubled people. This will also help you considerably in setting goals specific to the client's needs.

What skills do you need to become a life coach?

As a life coach, you need to have two primary skill sets: interpersonal, analytical and communication skills and professional skills.

The first skill set involves the following:

- Being passionate about helping other people to become achievers

- Having effective listening and questioning skills

- Being able to inspire and motivate other people

- Being able to be discreet, supportive and non-judgmental when listening to the life stories and aspirations of your clients.

Being passionate and confident enough in driving powerful, motivational and dynamic conversations with your clients during the entire life-coaching program.

The second skill set involves the following:

- Administration skills

- Financial and budgeting skills

- Time management skills

You can see that the last three items are items that need to be part of your practice simply from a practical business point of view. You will need to keep meticulous records, you will need to be able to balance your books and manage the time that you share between clients. Thus these are common sense skills that you would need for any kind of business that you decide to start. Training in these would be helpful because it would give you more time to concentrate on the actual coaching and less time on the mundane running of the business. You may also wish to employ someone in this capacity to free up your coaching time.

Should You Become a Life Coach?

So, how do you know that life coaching is the job for you? If you are still reading this book then you are in the right place for a start and you probably have some of the natural aptitudes that are required to be a successful life coach. That said, there are a number of specific skills that a life coach must have, including the following skills which are outlined in more detail:

- **Listening skills** – there is much more to listening than just hearing what a person is saying. One of the core skills required is the ability to hear what isn't being said. Reading between the lines and doing it accurately is essential because this feedback helps you to work out a program that is specifically designed to help your client to change their approach. If you don't have any idea of what that approach is – because you are too busy talking – then you need to practice effective listening skills.

- **Feedback** – you must be ready and prepared to give constructive feedback. There is a big difference between constructive feedback and negative criticism but the line between the two is also very thin. Being able to step on the right side of that line is critical to your success. If you are always pulling someone down for their errors, they are not likely to enjoy the experience or feel any enthusiasm for it. Instead, spread enthusiasm and make your clients want to achieve. That's half the battle with coaching.

- **Observing**. You must be able to see what isn't being said as well and being alert to any underlying factors that may be a root cause of the problem dictates your actions. The wrong assumptions may have negative consequences. Observation is one of the key points needed for coaching. You need to see beyond body language and be able to decipher what your client isn't telling you.

- **Analyzing** – Life coaches must be able to analyze information and draw their own valid conclusions from it before giving any advice or help with solutions. Entrepreneurs are very good at doing this, first drawing down the problem and then working on potential solutions until the right one to fit the circumstances as found. In your case, as a coach, it's the right one to fit the personality of your client that matters.

- **Communication** – You must be comfortable with communication, being able to get your point across and make yourself understood no matter whether you are face to face with your client, or on the telephone. Your own body language should inspire confidence and not leave a client doubting if you will be able to help.

- **Timing** – You must be aware of when your client is ready to move to the next stage of their development plan. The timing of this is critical – too soon and it will likely fail, too late and your client may lose confidence. You must always know the right questions to ask at the right time as well. Thus, having a plan drawn up for a client that has areas where assessment of the situation is done is vital to the overall success. These pinpoint areas of weakness and show areas where the client has fully understood. Thus, you don't need to waste time reinforcing things that you are sure they have learned and can use your time to reinforce those areas where there are still question marks.

- **Assimilation** – As a life coach you must be able to assimilate all your information into a workable plan. This goes without saying, but it's not as simple as you may think. You need a goal. You need to know exactly where your coaching is leading to get the client to the standard that they expect to be at by the end date. For an example, an Olympics athlete would expect his/her trainer to give training right up the event so that all training is done by the time the event arrives. It's much the same with relationship training and fitness training, as well as being able to work to a schedule with business trainees and financial clients. They want to see results.

- **Organizing** – Life coaches have to be organized. If you are not, you will get confused and so will your client. Keep all the information for each client separately and in an ordered fashion. I found from experience that this needs to be locked away or at least under a secure password if you use your computer to record your sessions. None of this information should be available to anyone but you and the client.

- **Empathy** – You must be compassionate and kind about the problems that your client is having and their needs in achieving their goals and overcoming the obstacles in their way. Did you know that being empathetic doesn't actually mean feeling sorry for your client? It means being able to put yourself in his/her shoes and that's a very different thing from being sorry for them.

25

- **Ethics** – You must maintain a code of ethics with your client and no divulge any of their information to anyone else. Confidentiality is a must for any life coach and respectful treatment of clients is a must.

- **Complimenting** – Don't hold back on complimenting your client when he or she deserves it. It makes the client happy and it boosts their confidence levels no end – for most of them, this is a major goal.

- **Motivating** – Life coaches should always be encouraging their clients, giving them motivation to continue with their plan and making them happy that they are doing the right thing. Be careful though – there is a fine line between sounding motivational and sounding patronizing.

- **Empowering** – Life coaches must empower their clients to move ahead with their goals and to succeed. This means making the client think rather than doing the thinking for them. Set them tasks that make them explore their responses because it's only by doing this that your client can advance.

- **Intuition** – Life coaches must demonstrate that they can read their gut feelings and act on them as well as communicating them. The more experience you have, the more this will help you with the work that you are undertaking.

- **Energetic** – Life coaches must have very high levels of vigor in order to properly motivate a client and this requires energy – lots of it. Your level of energy rubs off on the client and that's vital to success.

- **Positivism** – A life coach must have a positive attitude, a positive approach to their clients, a positive tone and must even be able to write positively. Positivisms spread to your clients, giving them an uplifting boost.

- **Creativity** – Life coaches have to be creative, as you will need to come up with several new ideas to give to your clients. One of the major roles of a life coach is the formation of ideas and putting them into practice tailored to the needs of the client.

- **Be Interested** – You have to be able to demonstrate that you are sincere and interested and absorbed in your clients and the success they must strive for. If you try to be too generic in approach, you will lose their confidence. Make sure that they know the program is tailored specifically for them. They want to feel they are getting your full attention, not just some printout that you use for everyone.

- **Self-Assured** – You must have the confidence in yourself to be able to make your life coaching conversations about the client, not about you. A self-assured life coach gives the client confidence and this confidence leads to trust which will help your cause.

- **Thirst for Knowledge** – In every meeting you have with a client there will be new things happening. There will always be something happening outside of your meetings as well and you must be familiar with and up to date with these things. Keep yourself updated with the latest research and familiarize yourself with new ideas and new areas that you come across. This will be of enormous help to your clients. I found with one particular client, she was experiencing something I had never come across before and upon researching it, I was able to expand on my methods to allow for cases such as hers. This was enormously helpful.

What are the working conditions of a life coach?

As a life coach, you will have a flexible working condition because you will be working with different clients in different locations. Most life coaches hold sessions with their clients in central locations that are quiet and conducive to discussions such as hotel lobbies and coffee shops. A meeting session can take around an hour where you need to encourage your client to openly talk about his or her life and aspirations. During your initial conversation with the client, you will start the process of aiding him or her in gaining proper perspective of his or her life, dreams and aspirations. You will have varying total number of life coaching hours with your different clients since they will have varying problems, issues and life goals that they want to achieve.

What work experience do you need to become a life coach?

In order to attract new clients, you will need to show an established track record in working with others in a coaching capacity. It is ideal if you have previous experience in training or handling other people. But if you don't have that experience, there is no need to worry. A lot of life coaches agree that one does not need to have any formal experience in working as a trainer, counselor or coach in order to become an effective life coach. What you need to have is expertise in the actual process of life coaching. Your own life experiences – both the good ones and the bad – are essential tools that can allow you to become effective in helping your clients achieve their own goals. Your goal setting must be specific. Clients will need to come away from each session with a goal in mind. As you get more experienced, you learn how high to set the goalposts for particular clients. If you set them too high, the client experiences disappointment and disillusionment. If you set them too low, you make your coaching too generic. Thus, working out strategies that make your client work are important.

When a teacher in a class teaches, they transfer information from their teaching to the student. Life coaching is much more complex than that. You not only impart information, but systems of logical sequence that help people aim toward specific goals. A teacher will teach and one and one equals 2. A life coach will teach how you get the initial one and add to it. All the processes that add dynamics to your client's life are dissected and systems are introduced which make those goals a lot more achievable. I remember one client saying that she wanted to be rich but when asking her "how rich" she had no idea. Thus, she had no target and could not possibly achieve her goal because it was unspecific. This is where life coaches make sense of what people actually want in their lives and help people to see those goals clearly. In relationship life coaching, many people had ideas about meeting their specific partner in life but they had no idea what their ideal was so were wasting time on people who were obviously not their ideal. By teaching specifics of goals, your clients are able to see the picture more clearly and stop wasting valuable time in their lives.

CHAPTER 3

Become Qualified

More and more people are making the choice to become a life coach in a bid to give their careers some direction. It is an interesting job, it's flexible, you can earn good money and you can work from your own home. However, that also means that everyone is doing it and a huge number of unscrupulous "trainers" have appeared on the scene, offering to make you into a life coach for the mere sum of just $500! Be careful that those who teach you are actually established in their field.

An overview of being a life coach is that a life coach is a person who works with a small handful of clients, giving them the help they need to get through a challenging part of their lives, through telephone conversations or face-to-face meetings. They may offer a one-off consultation or book a series of appointments to help with all different aspects of a client's life – perhaps relationships, personal or family, career choices, stress, managing time and more besides. They may also work with multi-media to try and advance their careers. If you want to produce videos, do you have the mindset? Do you want to employ someone to do this for you or is it something you need to learn?

It is worth bearing in mind that you do not need to have any formal qualifications to become a life coach. You do not have to fall for the hundreds of ads that appear in the backs of the newspapers or magazines, offering this course or that, and you do not need any official letters after your name to call yourself a life coach. However, clients may need to be assured of your qualifications if you are working with relationships and psychological problems that people have that stop them from making the most of their lives. You can't mess with people's minds and if they have psychological problems, qualifications help you to manage to set goals which help them to overcome those problems.

Most of the successful life coaches do have some kind of management training from a previous career, such as sports psychology or Neuro Linguistic Programming. Many of the sports or health and fitness life coaches are already qualified trainers or nutritionists. If you are working in the area of sports, your experience and reputation may mean that you need insurances to cover injury. Insurers may insist on knowing how qualified you are in that field of sports.

You must keep in mind that being a life coach is not something to be taken lightly. Previously, life coaches got a bad reputation with people saying that it was only those with too much time on their hands and no qualifications that became life coaches, telling people how to run their lives when they can't make a success on their own. That reputation has changed now because people expect more for the money they are paying out and life coaches have to know what they are doing and what they are saying is effective. Because of that, it is advisable that, if you are going to make a success of your new chosen career path, you should get some form of training under your belt.

College Education

A couple of decades ago, people could become well-known life coaches even if they only had high school education. But this has changed over more recent years. Because there is a lot of competition in the life coaching industry now, you need to have at least a four-year college degree in order for you to be at a par with other coaches. Many people will argue that one does not essentially have to have a college degree in order to become an effective life coach. However, since you will be dealing with different people, some of whom will have a Master's degree or doctorate, it is still ideal for you to have college education. Remember, people come from all walks of life and you need to be able to communicate with them in a way that they can relate to. Someone who is intellectual is not likely to relate to someone with very little education.

Life coaching is not yet offered as a degree in colleges and universities. But you can opt to get a degree in psychology or counseling in order to become a life coach. There are also certain universities who are now offering coaching programs that you can take. Some of these universities include University of Texas (both George Washington and Dallas), Harvard University, Penn State University, Yale, UC Berkeley, Duke, Georgetown and NYU.

Coaching Classes

You can also opt to take coaching classes that are offered in a number of accredited programs. The International Coaching Federation (ICF) and the International Association of Coaching (IAC) have partnerships with various schools that offer coaching classes that can help you become certified. You can check the websites of any of these two organizations to see if the school where you plan to enroll is an accredited partner. Do take your time checking because it's worth it to get a full education from professionals in this field, rather than opting to take courses that just fit in with your lifestyle, but have very little merit.

Certification

After you have successfully completed the coaching program, you will be eligible to become a certified life coach. You need to submit the requirements for certification to either the IAC or the ICF depending on which organization your school is affiliated with. After becoming certified, it will be easier for you to market your services to potential clients. Because of the stiff competition in the industry now, being certified can give you an edge against the other life coaches. Make sure that your certification is reflected in your business card and other marketing materials.

Continuous Learning

Your certification does not mean the end of your training. In order for you to become a true expert in life coaching, you need to get into the mindset of continuous learning. You need to make sure that you are always updated with the latest techniques in life coaching. One way to ensure this is by attending seminars given by credible institutions or speakers. Attending seminars is also a good way to build your network of people who can help you become successful in your career. For all you know, you will meet people during seminars who will be willing to become your mentor.

The other thing is that if you meet other life coaching experts, you may find that you can expand your business. Going to seminars will open up this avenue and give you an opportunity to work with others. That may increase your popularity and mean that you are able to work in various fields as a group, thus expanding the potential of your business. One coach that I know particularly well who started in relationship coaching went on to be a very busy and in demand business coach because her attitude meant that she didn't stop learning and seminars showed her that her approach was more flexible than others, thus allowing her to change the course of her career to one that she found more satisfying. You should never pigeonhole yourself or decide that you are only interested in one particular field. As a coach, you are growing as well as the client learning to reach his/her goals and your growth as a life coach may take you in directions you didn't expect. Thus, be flexible in your approach and open to learning new methods.

If you find that you are switching track, try neuro linguistic programming because this really will open you up to the possibilities that are out there for coaches. Even though my field is relationships, it made me understand how people think and how important empathy was to understanding the fuller picture and that's applicable to all kinds of coaching. If you are unable to put yourself in the client's shoes, how can you possibly see life from their perspective and correct that perspective? Neuro linguistic programming teaches you how to do this and it's extremely valuable for life coaches to learn. I know that when I took this course, I was doubtful about its usefulness to me, but I was completely wrong. It opens your mind to all kinds of things and the ideas that I now have are much more far reaching than they were before I took the course. Thus, if you do get an opportunity to take a course such as this, embrace it. It will make you stronger as a life coach in any field of work.

CHAPTER 4

What is a Life Coaching Business and What Are the Benefits?

Having your own life coaching business is the ultimate journey in self-improvement. You can't really master anything unless you have studied the client's wish list and wants and worked out a program that they can follow which will lead them there. When you become a life coach, you have to be able to show confidence and your clients will know if you are just faking it. Running your own business is a fantastic reason to have a really good life and to be happy and the greatest privilege is seeing the success, seeing your clients walk out of the door, standing taller, happier and more successful. When you see someone who is happy, you feel like you are achieving something fantastic, and that's when you know that you have helped him or her. When you see someone walk out of your office stronger, you feel stronger and this helps you to see the systems that are the most effective. You will experience all of the happiness, the joy and the fun that each and every client of yours feels. You will live their excitement and you will get to experience every second of joy they exude.

Of course, next to that is the feeling that you have helped them on their journey, that you have been at least partly responsible for the positive changes in their life. You will feel the gratitude that comes your way, and you will feel your own gratitude for having helped another person and for playing your part in making their world a much better place. It boosts your confidence but in a very positive way.

The third benefit is, of course, money, the good money you can earn from being a life coach. It may seem ridiculous that you can earn good money by working from a room in your own home, by picking up the phone and empowering people to change their own lives and to find success but you can. Next, I am going to tell you what a life coaching business is before I move on to telling you how to set yours up.

What is a Life Coaching Business?

When you set up your life coaching business, you are going to be guiding people in their lives, supporting them, counseling them and tracking their lives. As a life coach, you will work together with your client on virtually all areas of their life. Your job will be to:

- Make observations about your client, about what they are saying and be able to empathize and give feedback. This isn't advice. It's teaching them a new way of approaching life that will give them the results that they crave.

- Offer a plan that is relevant to the problems or issues that your client is experiencing which will give the client clear steps and goals that they have to meet in order to get to the next level.

- Follow your intuition and speak to it, as well as teaching your clients how to cultivate their own intuition. Many people don't even know what intuition is or how it helps them in the achievement of their goals.

- Come up with new ideas, possibilities and directions for your client to follow. This, to me, is the fun part. Just like a doctor prescribes medicines for physical illnesses, a life coach prescribes the approach that the client needs to take to improve that area of their life that is letting them down.

- Set up and hold strong accountability, from you and your client. Thus, you will need to have a very responsible attitude. If you have self-doubt, you cannot be a life coach.

- Give plenty of support to your clients. Share in their triumphs and share their triumphs if they are willing to give feedback that will help others to want to try your services. People like success and often those who gain from your coaching will be more than happy to show off their results, but do ask them.

Through all of this, you must be prepared to give freely to your client in a manner that always exceeds what your client could expect to receive from a family member or a friend. You must display an intensity and quality that is right for the circumstances and right for your client. A life coach goes beyond friendship. It is like stepping inside someone's head and reprogramming the way that they see the world and their approach to it.

Should You Start Your Own Life Coaching Business?

So, have you decided yet whether life coaching is the career path for you or are you still undecided? Ask yourself these questions and make a note of the answers:

- Is it vital that you do something to change the world? If you think that it is, then life coaching could be the answer. You have to want to make a difference and have to be enthusiastic about following it through.

- Do you get excited about the thought of helping someone who has a problem they can't get over or a goal they are struggling to attain, one that no one else has been able to help them with? If so, your chain of logic may be able to take that problem and make sense of it. It's extremely satisfying when you coach someone and see positive results.

- Do you have a fantastic life or are you looking for a way to improve on what you already have? In this case, you may need to work with people who already coach and who can show you methods that improve your life and also your approach to life coaching. Often life coaches learn from others. They have all the enthusiasm but don't have it channeled. By working with others, you learn a lot about putting together a whole package for a client. In the early days of my own career, I was asked to demonstrate the package proposed for a client based upon an interview and an assessment of what it was that they wanted to achieve.

- Do you like listening to other people talk about their problems, their dreams and goals? Do you know how to help channel people toward reaching those goals?

- Do you like giving impetus to other people? Half of the battle with coaching is making people see different approaches that actually improve the potential of improvement and development.

- Are you able to deal with rejection, at least rejection of the ideas that you come up with? You should always have a backup plan. A client may not respond to your suggestions or your program in the way that you envisaged. Thus flexibility is everything.

- Have you been through a good amount of life training or personal development training? Or are going through it now? You may need to use your experience to focus on the type of work that you want to do. Any training that you have will help you decide upon the market you are aiming for and thus help you to target that audience.

- Do you like the idea of a pure service business? Remember, what you will be selling as a coach are ideas. You are selling a package but it's not a tangible package. It's more complex than that. The service that you do for your clients is use methods to help them see things in a way that helps them to develop in their lives to the extent that they envisaged when they hired you.

- Are you prepared to show creativity in your business plan, instead of having a standard one, to make your business successful? Flexibility is one of the main things that a life coach is able to work with. Because their range of experience should be varied, their approach to problems will often be the unexpected approach and people may need a certain amount of convincing that this is the way to make dreams happen.

If you could answer yes to most, if not all, of these questions then you are ready to get on the path to your own success by starting up a life coaching business. It's clear that this is what you are destined to do and there is little point in waiting around. Once you have set your business up, be prepared to:

- Start calling people and spreading the word

- Set up free coaching sessions to get testimonials, feedback and experience

- Sign up those paying clients based on those testimonials

- Start designing courses for life coaching, as these are helpful to gain money from groups of people.

- Set up your business marketing plan and get all the materials you need. That includes videos, social marketing tools and of course your website.

You will enjoy some of these activities and you will find others a challenge. Remember that solving a problem creatively is what it's all about and making your coaching individual and unique. The following steps are the six steps that you need to take to start up a successful life coaching business.

The Seven Stages of a Successful Life Coaching Business

There are seven growth stages you need to go through when you are starting up your own life coaching business. Each stage has its own goals, activities and skills that you need to learn to be successful:

Preparation Stage

This stage is optional and you may not need to do it. That will depend on your personal development level. In the preparation stage, you are going to need to prepare yourself and your own life to become a successful life coach for other people. Part of this requires making sure you have your head firmly screwed on and know exactly what you are getting into. The second part is making sure your life is firmly on track – if it isn't, now is the time to get it sorted. If you bring your problems to the table you cannot devote the time that you need or the concentration that you need as a life coach.

This does not mean that you have to take up Buddhism or go out and achieve something that very few people have (a perfect life). Far from it, what this means is that you need to get your mind, body and intellect honed so that your personal life does not interfere with your work. Clients are depending on you and you can't just make excuses once you take on a client. You may need to make some major changes and you may need to get yourself on some coaching and training courses to make sure you can get through this stage successfully.

Stage One: Learning

In this stage, you are going to be doing a lot of learning. You will need to learn the skills necessary to coach other people, and you need to learn how to apply those skills in the real world, in real-life scenarios. You may get away with just a bit of practice with a friend or win a training circle or you may need to go on a proper course but this is the stage where you really **begin** coaching people. This is also the time to get any reading or studying done in preparation for the next stage and where you would gain the correct certifications to be a life coach. Everything that you learn will help you. For example, attending conferences and watching other life coaches in action is extremely helpful because it shows you the level at which you will be expected to perform when dealing with your client base.

Stage Two: Launch

This is the time to announce to the world what your intentions are. This is where you tell everyone that you are a life coach and then you start to act on your intentions. This is where you begin networking, marketing, selling yourself as a coach and where you begin to build your business up. This could the hardest stage for you because this is the time when people are going to doubt your abilities, doubt whether you are serious about being a life coach. It is up to you to prove them wrong. Remember, as outlined several times within this book, you need to have given free consultations to get those testimonials rolling in. People won't believe what you say you can offer unless you can back it up with results.

Stage Three: One-On-One Coaching

In this stage you will start to get into your groove, you should be picking up new clients on a reasonably consistent basis as well as hanging on to a high percentage of them for the long run. This is the time for you to work out:

- Where your leads are going to come from and how to increase the amount of leads that you have. Remember, spreading the word is essential and your website needs to be developed as shown in a later chapter.

- How you are going to get your free session clients to sign up for paid coaching sessions. This is relatively easy. The free sessions should be limited to a certain duration only and should present the client with obvious positive results, using the "carrot" to tempt them into what you have on offer for them if they want to enroll.

- How you are going to keep your clients coming back to you for years. You actually form some pretty strong bonds over the years and many will want to be a part of your career, just as you want them to be a part of yours. Cash in on this idea.

- How to manage the administration and financial side of your business and manage your client relationships. Client relationships should always be handled by you as they will expect to, but you can hand admin jobs to someone else who can work behind the scenes. You can also use them to deal with answering emails, writing up pages for your webpage and making sure that people get timely responses from your webpage.

In this stage, a good life coach could reasonably expect to earn up to $7000 a month just by coaching clients on a one to one basis

Stage Four: Group Coaching

In this stage, you will be working out how to improve on everything that you mastered in the one to one stage, improve to the level that you can coach groups of clients and still get the results you want. This is where you need to:

Pick up even more leads to get your groups filled up. Use specific goals to get clients. Target your audience and show them by the title of your courses what the course has on offer that they want.

Improve your skills as a coach and do better than ever before. It's always worth being boastful about your clients. That means saying how happy you are with your client's progress. One life coach that I know well uses this as a real pull for new clients. She always does so using the client's permission but is quick to tell everyone what a client has achieved and what they can achieve if they attend the courses.

Improve on your client relationship management skills. This is vital as if you lose clients, you may also stand to lose your reputation and that is paramount to success.

A successful coach in this stage, one who really knows what he or she is doing, could make from $10,000 to $100,000 per month, although don't expect this to happen – if it does, see it as the bonus it is and learn to teach others to develop their skills and ambitions as well.

Stage Five: Guru Level Coaching

This is where you are going to take all of the knowledge that you have learned and gained while coaching individuals and groups and turn it all into a top class product. This will be a product that you can sell, on the Internet or during those speaking engagements you will be invited to. You will also probably find yourself in demand to carry out workshops and training sessions so be prepared.

This is where you find that you can help more people by selling your products and your training sessions to your clients and other leads. And you will likely pick up even more clients for your group or individual coaching sessions. Conferences, seminars and speaking engagements which are high profile and have high profile people attending will add to your credibility and help you to develop to the stage where you can actually ask top quality wages based on your reputation and your ability to deliver.

Stage Six: Business Building

If you have made it to this stage then well done! This is where you are going to build your team, your business and you are going to turn all that you have learned and all that you have accomplished in the first five stages and turn it into a truly successful business. This is where:

- Your business team will work hard to develop your product and your training sessions. It's good to mix with a team because team ideas can be more innovative and can be incorporated into your coursework and seminars.

- Your team will hold the group and individual coaching sessions and will all be trained to work in a set manner that fits with your reputation. That's important. If they want to freelance at a later date that is up to them but if you are investing in a team, your image is everything to the public. Be sure not to take on dead wood.

- Your team will run the administration side of your business, the sales and the marketing campaigns and will attend regular meetings to come up with ideas for expanding your business. Web development, video presentation and keeping up with the competition will all be part of their research and development tasks.

You can do exactly as you choose to, rather than having to work every single day to keep the money coming in. A coach that gets to this stage can make as much money as he/she wants, and can work when they feel like it and take time off when they do not. However, be sufficiently present to make sure that your team are using the philosophies that you have specifically taught them to use and that there are no complaints from clients who feel they are not getting what they are paying for.

The point of life coaching is passing your expertise to others who will gain from it. On the pages of Facebook, you find many life coaches who travel the world and do exactly what they want to do because they have found the secret of using their personalities to improve the lives of others. However, do bear in mind that many work very long hours through choice because there are so many life coaches in the business now that sometimes you have to do this to get to the stage when you can feel confident with what you are offering the public and know that it's the best service that they can get.

If this is something that you think you would like to do, remember that you need to follow the blueprint shown in the next chapter to actually set yourself up as a life coach. It's worthwhile as a profession but it's also something that takes a lot of dedication. Life coaching isn't just a question of standing in front of an audience and speaking. It's about being so confident with what you are offering that clients jump at the chance of being part of what you promise to add to their lives.

CHAPTER 5

Looking at the Blueprint of Life Coaching

To find your way around the maze that takes you into life coaching, you need to consider the following. These are all important for their own reasons. Before you can even consider setting up your company, you have to have worked on the idea so that what you present to potential clients shows what they will get for their money. While some coaches find that their career evolves simply due to their past experience, such as sports coaches who used to be well known sports personalities, etc., most people don't have a public face already, so you need to create one. You can't offer your services, if you can't show an example of what you are able to offer people. This is the blueprint to success:

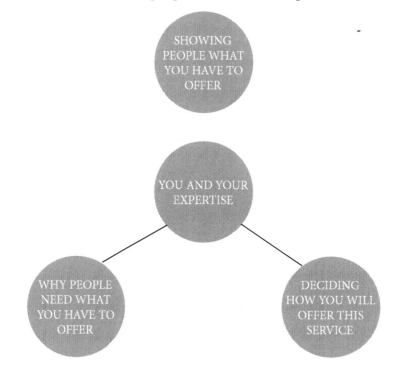

If you look at the above diagram, you will see that you need a clear idea of what you have to offer, how you are going to offer it, why people need what you have and actually deciding how to show people. That's a whole load of stuff to decide. So, supposing I wanted to offer life coaching to people who suffered bereavement, using the above outline, I can come up with the following answers:

- I will offer bereavement life coaching

- People need this because grief is a hard thing to handle

- I will prepare videos that will introduce my services

- I will need a website, where people can enroll for help

- I will need to prepare video content and articles for that website

- I will need to liaise with people in places where people are likely to be dealing with loss

- I will need to set a charge for the service offered.

In this case, you are dealing with the emotional side of life coaching, but there's actually much more to it than that. People who look for bereavement life coaching are actually looking for a new way forward in their lives and that's what you are offering them – a little hope in a doom and gloom life changing situation. It's not about taking advantage of people. It's about offering them an alternative way forward that will enrich their lives.

All of this looks straightforward so far, but what about the other things that come into the picture? How am I going to offer those services? Knowing that I am one individual and that I can't afford to employ others, how am I going to fix it up so that I have enough time on my hands to actually deal with the demand that is likely? This is something that can be programmed easily once you are organized and even part time help can assist you. There are loads of people who are searching for work online and remote help can be a lot cheaper than actually hiring staff so do look into it.

Thus this gives you the purpose for having outlets that are useful to people while you are too busy to answer questions. Having a website, sending out newsletters about conferences that you are likely to speak at and sharing the news via social media may help you to spread out what you are able to offer people.

One life coach that I am very familiar with uses Facebook as a platform to spread news, but backs that up with a written book and glowing testimonials from businesses and individuals she has helped to reach their potential. Life coaching is about helping people to get beyond the knowledge they have and learn to get more out of life, no matter what the circumstances. Thus, if you have pre-prepared materials, these can be used to help spread the word via sites such as YouTube, Facebook or by using contacts through your website. Your website will therefore need to encourage people to want to know more about the services that you offer and since this will provide you with clients should reflect the kind of service you can help people with.

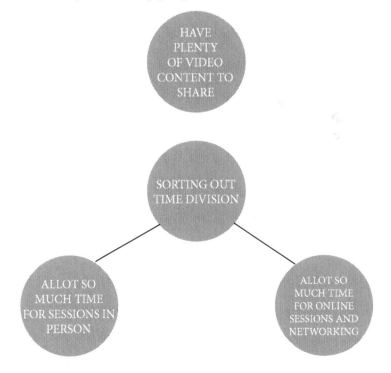

That looks fairly straightforward but if you want to get your name spread around, you also have to look at social media, potential lectures that you can give which will in turn generate more interest from the public and make yourself available to referrals from organizations that have people with problems that need help. All the video content that you have and website articles that you use free up your time to be doing other things. You may even have to give free advice to get clients to stick with you or to tempt a client to use your services on a regular basis.

In a business environment you need to decide, for example, what you have on offer and what advantage it would be to those who are seeking help with staff training. Approaching the CEO of a company with a vague idea about what you have on offer isn't enough. You need to be able to show the company what you do and explain how it helps the work environment to become more productive. People don't hire life coaches just because it's the trendy thing to do. They want to be sure that what you offer be worth it.

For life coaches who take on health associated coaching, it's important that you prepare a wide range of video content and podcasts that you can refer potential clients to, in order to demonstrate exactly what you have to offer. You must have seen the adverts for slimming pills. The first thing that the adverts do is compare someone before and after – and often the images that you see are not that honestly presented, but they are serving a purpose. Girl A weighs too much and knows it. She sees a photo a girl B on the advert. She's not a particularly pretty girl and that makes Girl A feel comfortable that this can work for anyone. Thus, she is enticed into trying whatever is on offer that girl B seems to have achieved, whether this is weight loss, lack of wrinkles, firm body or agility. The Photos that you see on websites giving before and after lure people into buying the product. In the same way, if you are offering services to benefit people's health, you need to lure people into hiring you. There are several ways that this can be done.

The Lure

On the website, there can be testimonials from people who have used your services and whose lives have improved because of those services. That's pretty much the same as the before and after photographs, but the problem may be that you don't actually have a client base to get those testimonials from. In this case, offer your services free for a limited period of time before you actually set up business and use these clients for the testimonials. Why will they give you great references? Because you gave them a great service for nothing! That's really good lure to get those testimonials rolling in. You have to start somewhere and tempting people because they read other people's results is a first rate way.

You also need to send a clear message to readers of your website and postings that you make on the Internet just what's in it for them. People are not going to hire you just because you say you're good at what you do. They need to see what benefits can be had from hiring you or your associates and that's where you can add events that you have taken part in and show pictures of people with the testimonials of what they actually gained from using you for life coaching.

The particular life coach that I am familiar with really does plug herself on Facebook and tells people that they are not living up to their potential. They can have a villa in paradise and the best car out there, but they need to know how to actually visualize a difference in their lifestyle and apply certain tactics in order to achieve these things. They are great pullers of supporters. Other life coaches teach single people to get in touch with their soul mate, simply by changing their behavior. You need to lure people. If, for example, you are a business life coach, show businesses why they need your savvy and what it will mean to their business because the bottom line with all of this kind of work is always going to be "What's in it for me?"

Endorsements from people who are well known are also very useful. If you can arrange to attend events where you know that there are well known personalities in the same field as you lecture or coach, then these are great events for circulating and getting your name out there with the best in the business.

So far, we have discussed the blueprint but the blueprint isn't ready until the video content or written documentation and website are produced and presented to people. Don't go amateur. What happens when you present a badly produced video is that you make people question your ability to coach them. What they want to see is genuine professionalism. Be slick but be honest. Write out and rewrite your scripts and get professional people to make the videos. It costs more, but you don't end up with an amateur video telling people how to live their lives when you don't even seem to have the money to present yourself and your ideas well. There are loads of personal coaching videos on YouTube. Study the competition. See what you can offer that they are not offering. Monetize your video content and link it to your website. Make sure that your literature is out there for people to buy and instead of plumbing to sell it privately only, make sure you are listed on major websites such as Amazon as well because you may gain even more clients from doing so.

Your written material and even your scripts need to make you look like you know how to use all the techniques of self-development and impart that knowledge to others. The psychology behind this kind of work suits a character who is charismatic and who can pass ideas to another human being and make that human being see life from a different perspective. For example, in business life coaching, often neuro linguistic ideas are practiced which gives people an overview of situations where other cultures or ideas are concerned. This is a very satisfying and rewarding style of life coaching for those whose minds are able to put things in neat little boxes but your videos and your presentation articles on the website have to pass the right message without looking corny or hackneyed. People don't want a good salesman any more. They want someone who understands how to develop personal growth and demonstrate how to use this within their lives to make their lives richer, make them more efficient and also to put life into some kind of perspective, where goals are more defined and thus easier to work toward.

Although further chapters go into setting up the business, you really need your head screwed on the right way to see what personal development means to the individual and what their expectations of you will be. Work out what the goal of the sessions will be because people want to walk away from sessions feeling like they have actually gained something. If they don't, you will fail so before you are able to get your business rolling, you need to set out your aims, get your literature and website ready and not actually go forward on anything but a private basis just until you have sufficient references to add weight to what you offer.

CHAPTER 6

Gathering Up Information To Make Your Business Work

When people seek out the help of a life coach, they do so for a specific reason. People get stuck in their lives in certain areas and a life coach helps them to be responsible for developing that area so that their life is more satisfying. Let's give you a few examples:

Weight loss life coach – This is someone who makes you accountable for what you eat by setting you goals and making sure that you keep to them. It's not about giving advice. It's about making someone accountable for what may be going wrong in their lives. For this example, the life coach teaches the client about nutrition but it doesn't stop there. They are challenged to try new things and to experiment with different foods and varieties of foods and to report back on their process. In fact, chances are that if you took on a life coach for this very purpose, it's because you don't have the discipline and are crying out for help. People don't generally take on a life coach in any area of their lives without being deadly serious about getting results. A pep talk doesn't do it. It's not about holding someone's hand. It's about teaching them to use every bit of power within them to solve their own problem.

Thus, you need to gather sufficient information and have sufficient persuasion tactics to make someone look at their life in a different way, giving them challenges that will check on the progress that they are making. Yes, common sense will come into it, but life coaching is more than that. It's all about teaching someone to see things from another perspective and actually achieve. Thus, you need to be ahead of other coaches and come up with more unique challenges that really will prove your worth. Look at advertising in this field. Read up what your competition is offering and make sure that the information that you gather is more comprehensive and offers the client more.

On your website, you will need more than just a lure. You will need to spell out a certain amount of what you do, without giving too much away. Life coaches tend to show people what they have on offer but are very secretive about the methods that will be employed to achieve the results that they boast. Also look at how websites lure people because this is vital to success. One well known website offers life coaching online, and their website spells out what you may be looking for asking it in question format. What's clever about this particular lure is that the website owners have managed to add Join Now links all the way through the script without actually interfering with the flow of the website and people are encouraged to have a free session. That's a really good way of selling yourself. Thus, this chapter is about gathering information pertaining to your services. How can you sell yourself? What would you want to give for free? How do you set up your session fees? What can people expect to get for those fees and what will you offer as the "carrot" or answer the question of "what's in it for me?"

Information that you may wish to check on is which kind of service do you want to use? There are several choices available to life coaches these days. For example, if you are offering online life coaching, you need to choose a means to communicate with clients. Skype and Google Hangouts are possibilities but you need to be totally conversant with these services and learn to present yourself in a manner that looks like you know what you're doing. Find out what backdrop will help you. I use these services all of the time because they give me a chance to get up close and personal with clients. The relationships clients that I work with are the type of people who need that contact. It gives them trust in me and helps them to see me as a human being who is prepared to listen, but who is also able to empathize and that's vital to those who decide to work with relationships or with any kind of life coaching that involves emotions.

By using these media, you are able to get your clients to open up and tell you what it is that they are aiming for. Don't put words into their mouths. Don't suggest the course that their life should take. Learn to listen because listening is the most important skill to life coaching. Sometimes, I have sessions and I drop small hints and ask them to give me feedback from specific words. These words are tailored to see what their thinking processes are, but also to help me glean a clear picture of who these people are and what they expect to get from me. If you give your own ideas to them, they may be disappointed and feel overwhelmed. If you let them tell you what their problems are, you gear your sessions around their needs rather than thinking that what you think they should do takes precedence. It doesn't. Life coaching is teaching people to achieve for themselves what **they** actually want to achieve.

Extras

You also need to know what widgets to add to your website. These are little buttons where people can share the page that they access if they feel that it would be something of interest to a friend. Do your investigation. Learn how to use all these possibilities before you go live and start giving paid sessions. You need some kind of feedback on what your presentation is like and perhaps you have friends who will be able to give you honest feedback.

CHAPTER 7

Set Up Your Life Coaching Business

Don't let go of your stable job just yet.

It is easy to become a certified life coach. But earning a decent income as a life coach will not happen overnight. Most often than not, many life coaches need to build their credentials for several years before they can build a strong client base and start charging decent rates. You cannot really expect to receive a lot of calls from prospective clients, right after getting your certification. This means that you will not be able to rely on your life coaching income alone to pay for your living expenses such as rent, utilities and groceries. Some life coaches even give out free consultations and coaching sessions in order to build their network and gain experience. This means that you need to ensure that you have another source of stable income while you are building your career in life coaching. If you find an opening where you will be able to develop your life coaching, that's the ideal because you will be able to branch out on your own later on or might not even want to. Some agencies that employ life coaches are so encouraging and give such good wages that you don't want to go independent for a while. You may even find yourself going into partnership with other life coaches eventually.

Self-employment

There are several life coaches who are directly employed by corporations who have their own coaching department for the training requirements of their employees. But the majority of life coaches are actually self-employed. As such, you need to acquaint yourself with the business requirements for self-employment. Aside from being familiar with your tax obligations, you also need to juggle different roles that come with business operations. You will manage your client schedules, invoicing, and even the finances of your "business." Of course, you always have the option of hiring an assistant and a bookkeeper to help you but while you are still building your client base, you may need to handle all these roles by yourself. Any extra cost means that you have more obligations during a time that you have no guaranteed income. Believing in your abilities isn't enough at this stage of the game, so be prepared to work hard. Self-employment costs money and you need to find out what the rules are particularly if you decide to use your skills over the Internet.

Get a mentor

You cannot really learn all the tricks of the trade just by becoming a certified life coach. It is ideal if you can get a mentor who has adequate experience and who can teach you the best practices in life coaching. If you are lucky enough to be friends with expert life coaches, do not hesitate to seek their help. Remember, truly great people are not selfish with their knowledge. If your circle of friends does not include an expert life coach, you can always ask your school to see if they can recommend a mentor for you. You can ask your classmates or teachers for any recommendation. If all else fails, you can always look at directories to talk to enlisted life coaches and see if there is someone who can help you. Mentoring can be done either on a one on one basis or as a group. Choose the format that suits your personality and learning style.

One of the benefits of being mentored is that you will see from a practical point of view how life coaching really works. Always keep in mind that life coaching is a profession that requires skills and techniques. And many of these skills and techniques are not in born. You need to spend enough time to learn and practice them. Having a mentor, your own life coach, can help you achieve your goal of becoming an effective life coach a lot faster.

Be aware that this may cost money. One thing you can do is to offer your services on a part time basis with your mentor for free – perhaps helping them with things that they need help with, but keep up your full time employment to make sure that you have enough to put food on the table. Approach several potential mentors and see what they offer in the way of help to new people setting up as a life coach. The coaching network online is quite useful and there are country based sites that help life coaches to get started. The nice thing about the coaching network is that they do have forums where mentors and coaches can get together and ask questions and that's useful for you because it gives you an opportunity to read the answers to other people's questions about this kind of business. Those answers may give you more information than you could possibly hope for in one place. It also helps because it puts you in touch with the right kind of people and even helps in getting a clientele base set up.

Enlist yourself in online coaching directories

There are a number of life coaching directories on the Internet where you can have your services listed. A lot of people are now turning to the Internet to look for professional life coaches who can help them with their personal and professional goals. You will be able to reach more people by listing yourself in online directories. The majority of the online life coaching directories will require you to pay a certain amount in order for you to create your profile in their directory. Before you pay them with your hard earned money, do some research first to make sure that you are not dealing with a company that is less than professional or scamming people trying to set up a business, knowing how keen they are to get their name out there. If you use Google, and then type in "Life Coaching Directory" there are plenty listed that you can add your name to.

Define your niche market

Life coaching has become a very huge industry. There was a report in 2012 in the New York Times where the writer was a little skeptical about the expertise of some of the online life coaches or the courses that were available and it found that many of these were inexperienced people in their mid-twenties. Although this may have given people cause for concern, one of the things said in that report was interesting and came from a top life coach, who backed up young people choosing to go into that particular profession. Hugo Cory whose earnings are very good and established said that he admired these young coaches and also said that if you were not meant to be a coach, you won't get the clientele. The thing that is interesting is that universities are beginning to see the power of coaching and are offering courses now to young people that may help them to establish themselves as professionals with impressive credentials. One effective way for you to make your mark is to define your own niche market.

Do you want to become a life coach who specializes in coaching people on how to define their visions and how to look for ways to improve their overall approach to life? Do you want to become a life coach who focuses on assisting clients select the right career for them and training for their chosen career? Do you want to be a life coach who helps business executives in running their operations? Or do you want to be a life coach who helps clients manage their interpersonal relationships? The niche market that you should choose should be something that you have an expertise on. It can be something that you yourself excel in. Here are some of the niche markets that you can choose from:

- Work/life balance coaching

- Business coaching

- Weight and body image coaching

- Carbon coaching (wherein you will help clients lessen their carbon footprint)

- Time management coaching

- Career coaching

- Spiritual coaching

- Corporate coaching

- Retirement coaching

- Executive coaching

- Relationship coaching

Remember, if you don't have sufficient experience in your field, you will probably not do well. You need to have at least studied the area you want to begin life coaching in and should be able to show from your free interview initially with clients that you are who you say you are and have the expertise that you claim to have. Most people can see through those that are inexperienced and that do not give them confidence within that first session, which is why it's important to choose the right niche.

Build your marketing program.

After you have become certified in life coaching, you need to let other people know about your life coaching services. You can do this by creating a marketing program that can involve getting online or newspaper ads, handing out business cards, creating a Facebook page and other social media accounts, creating a blog and writing in community journals and pages. Your objective is to have name recognition so that potential clients know that you exist.

If you have already identified your niche market, you should market yourself as a specialist or an expert in that niche. You need to know what kind of materials your target clients like to read, listen to or view. If you want to target business executives, you need to find ways to reach them. If you want to target housewives or career women, you need to customize your marketing program to get in touch with them.

Research studies show that coaching is not only beneficial to employees but to employers, as well. It has been shown that business organizations that spend at least $1 on the well being of their employees (including coaching and other trainings) are able to have at least $3 savings because of lower turnover and improved performance. You can use these facts when selling your services to business owners or business executives.

Offer Your Services for Free

After you have become certified, you will need some clients you can work with to build your experience. But without any previous life coaching experience, it may be hard for you to look for potential clients willing to pay you to coach them. What you can do to build your experience is to offer your life coaching services to your family and friends for free. This has two benefits: you will be able to have life coaching hours under your name and you will be able to help someone close to you achieve their goals.

You can decide how many free coaching sessions you will give and how long you want to do these free services. You need to always assess yourself to know if you have already become more confident in your own skills and techniques or you need more "practice". Some life coaches only give free services for a couple of weeks while others give them for as long as a year. But you need to make sure that you are not just giving the excuse "I am not yet ready" for delaying your plans. Always remember that becoming an expert in life coaching will require a lot of years. At some point, you need to decide that you are ready to take on the real thing. Use these learning approaches to help you to see where you are going wrong. If you have the means to record your voice during the initial meetings this will be really helpful. Just as body language matters when you are on a stage, when you put yourself in front of a laptop camera to talk to clients, you have to have the right presence. Listen to your recordings – work out where you stutter, where you sound unsure, where you sound unprofessional. As a life coach, would you have persuaded the client with the demeanor that the recording shows?

Your free services can't really be complained too much about, but these give you a wonderful opportunity to shine and to learn about what you may be doing wrongly. A doctor, for example, doesn't learn bedside manners until he is in a hospital environment and even then he may get it wrong. This initial period is to help you to achieve your own goals as well as helping clients to achieve theirs. You have to be convincing. You have to be able to enforce goals and expect results from your clients, giving them tasks to do to ensure that they have fully understood the processes that you are introducing. You are not teaching. You are coaching which means you are encouraging them to change their behaviors to gain progress in the way that they wish to.

Start getting real clients

If your first clients who received your services for free are happy with your life coaching, it is highly likely that they will tell other people about you. Eventually, your name and what you do will reach more people through word of mouth. During this time, you may start receiving calls from potential clients who are interested in working with you. This is a good way to market yourself but now is also the best time to implement the marketing program that you have planned before. If you need to, start looking for a business coach who can help you implement your marketing strategies.

One of the things that you need to carefully think about is pricing. What will be your rate? How much will you charge your clients? Will you give daily rates or monthly rates? Will you give different rates for different people? If someone who is deep in debt wants to work with you, how much will you charge that person? Are you willing to do it for free while your client is getting over his or her financial issues and just collect your fees when your client is more financially stable?

Here is where a mentor will come in handy. It is ideal if you can get advice from people who have years of experience in life coaching. It is also important that you set your fees based on results and not based on the actual number of hours or days that you worked with the client. Do not consider offering your services for a cheap fee just in order to get clients from your competitors. This is not how life coaching works. Work with your mentor in plotting your life coaching business.

Always ask your satisfied clients if they will be willing to give testimonials that you can use in marketing your services to potential clients. Another good marketing strategy is to offer potential clients a coaching session for free to see if they will like your coaching style. Most life coaching websites do this. This also gives you and the client a chance to meet and to see if you can work together. It doesn't happen often, but occasionally you get a client that you know that you will not be able to help. In a case like this, don't pretend about it just for the money. If you don't think that your style of coaching will work with a particular individual, don't take them on. It can only make your reputation worse as they will undoubtedly be disappointed with your services.

One potential client that I had told me that she had been through about 8 different coaching services and was thoroughly disgusted with the fact that they didn't live up to promise. I asked her whether she had kept her side of the bargain by actually doing the homework she was given and the look on her face was such that I knew she had not. I explained to her what life coaching was. It wasn't a case of teaching her. It was a case of using methods that helped her to develop her own approach. It seemed that no one had actually explained this to her, or if they had, it had fallen on deaf ears. She thought that she was paying for a service and as such that the coach should do everything, rather than it affecting her outlook on life. If you find a client that doesn't understand what you do, don't take them on until you have given them a good overview or you may be setting yourself up with disappointment.

General Tips

When you first start up your life coaching business you are going to have a lot of questions that you want the answers to. While I can't possibly answer all your questions here, I can give you some general tips on how to get going – some of this is just reiterating what I have already said but I consider it important enough to tell you again. You will also need to understand that clients often need the whole picture explaining to them. That's why your website appearance is so important. It builds up client expectation and their expectations of you should be realistic. For example, if you promise someone you will give them the means to become a millionaire, then they are going to expect that. If you promise them that you can show them how to make their lifestyle the one that they want, they will expect that to happen. If you know that your methods will allow that to happen, then you really don't have any problem. If you think that by the end of the course they won't have any better an idea, then you have your work cut out for you. To change the way that people think, you have to make them see things from a different viewpoint and some are just plain difficult.

Make this your side job – do not, under any cir
your main job straightaway. Building up a new v.
one such as life coaching takes time and effort, not to menu
If you quit your main job, you will have plenty of time on your ha.
but not the money and there are no guarantees that you are going to
be successful right off the bat. Do not risk your house if you have
a mortgage on it on the basis that you think you are going to earn a
fortune. It takes a while to actually build up a clientele base and you
should think of your initial outing into life coaching as helping you to
build on your experience so that when you actually do go full time,
you are sure that you can demand a reasonable hourly rate and expect
clients to accept that as the going rate.

Keep some cash to one side to pay for your certifications. Although
you do not have to do this, you should. It will make your business
far more credible if you can show your clients that you are certified
to be a life coach. Life coaching training has an awful lot going for it
and you can learn about so many different tools of the trade that you
would be stupid not to do it. Look into University courses as well.
As stated earlier, sometimes these can add a lot of weight to your
business, especially since Universities have now started to take this
kind of business very seriously and are offering good quality courses
that cover different types of life coaching.

Try to work with someone. If you can, get someone in to help even if it
is a virtual assistant. You will need help with the marketing side of the
business, your social media presence, designing a kick-ass website,
even someone to babysit for you when time demands it! You can do
it alone if you want to, but my advice is not to, it will be much harder
work. I actually believe that a life coach needs to be single minded
and that means that it is actually better to do this when there are not
pressing family obligations in the background. Some people can
manage it, but it's unlikely to make you a fortune if you have to keep
stopping to look after a baby. That's not to say that you can't. Some
life coaches manage to couple the two activities very well indeed, but
it's beyond me how they manage. In my job, I am busy for most of my
waking hours and I don't think that having young kids to look after

would be viable in a case such as mine.

- Focus on one thing at a time. Especially when you are just starting out. It's so easy to get over excited and put all your energy into trying to do everything, but believe me, you will go crazy and you will achieve little. Unless you have hired people to help you out, you simply cannot do it all at once. Take it one step at a time and focus on one thing at a time. This means deciding upon what your specialty is. You cannot possibly learn all the methods that you will need to deal with all kinds of life coaching. Thus, find out what you want to do and stick to it, making sure that you put all your energy into that field of coaching. If you diversify too much, it actually takes your attention off what you are doing and makes it too bitty.

- Don't expect to be a success overnight – it isn't going to happen. As with most businesses, life coaching can take many years before you will see any real success. It is no good comparing yourself to other life coaches and bemoaning the fact that you are not as successful as they are. No one ever gained overnight success and most of these people have taken years to get to where they are now. Your best friends from here on are patience and persistence. You have to ask yourself how badly you want this job and how far you are prepared to go to get it. If you are determined, single minded and able to understand how life coaching works, you could be great, but you don't get there overnight. Use this time to develop your image because your image is everything.

- Never give up. Following on from persistence, you are going to experience setbacks in your career and that's a given. You will have days, even weeks or months where nothing seems to go right. The trick is not to give up or give in. With a life coach business, you have to stick it out for at least a year, if not two, to see any real progress. To be fair, it may even be three years of solid hard work before you start to see the profit you hoped to gain. Those first few years are going to see you paying out more than you are bringing in on occasion as you set up the marketing and social media side of the business. Don't worry, eventually they will pay for themselves but this is why you should not give up your main job straight away.

- Do what feels right. Even if it's the polar opposite of what everyone else seems to be doing, you should always do what you think or feel is the right this. There is no set way; no perfect way to do these things, the only way for you is your way. This will include the methods that you learn when you take qualifications but a good quality life coach will devise their own methods based upon this learning. There are some steps that you do need to take to gain clients, the right kind of clients but you don't have to copy the blueprint of some- one else's business. Sometimes doing what is different may be the one thing that pulls the clients in, simply because they are looking for something different. The ultimate aim of the client is the first consideration, rather than how slick you present yourself. You need to give clients 100 percent reassurance that what they want to achieve is possible and know how they can achieve it.

- Keep in mind that this is not a get rich quick scheme. Nor is it an easy way to make a living. No self-run business is easy. Not only do you have to find the money to start up, you have to market your business effectively – that takes time and money – you have to take the time out to create your niche in the market and work out how to bring the clients in. No, this is far from being easy but it is an amazing job, you do get to help other people and you can leave your desk every day with deep satisfaction, knowing that you have helped, if only in a small way, to make things better for another person. I saw one life coach on Facebook giving the impression that anyone could live in a tropical paradise and not have to work, that they could travel the world and do whatever they wanted to do and were only held back by their imaginations. However, if you are promising a client a result, you need to make that result depend upon their total cooperation and understanding of your methods.

Passion wins out in the end. Do not go into this line of business if you have no passion for the work. Yes, sure, you'll have times when it all goes to hell in a hand basket and things don't look too rosy but everyone has days like that, no matter what line of business they are in. Sheer passion for the work will win through but if you do not have that then look elsewhere. It's you passion for the work that will come across to your clients – they deserve it and if you can't give it, turn away now.

CHAPTER 8

Find Effective Ways to Work With Your Clients

Begin with a thorough interview

You cannot really claim that you will be able to determine the problems of a client just by looking at him or her or listening to a short introduction. Your first sessions with your clients should always involve a thorough interview to better understand him or her from different perspectives. You need to learn about their expectations from your life coaching sessions. You need to learn which specific areas of their lives they need you to help develop. There are cases when they are seeking help in their career when the real issues are in their family life. You need to determine what their true desires and aspirations really are. Here is where your listening skills will be most useful. This initial meeting with a client tells you a lot of things and your listening skills are vital as well as being able to read their body language. You may see instantly why they are failing, but unless you listen to the client and read between the lines, you won't be able to provide the service that they are expecting. Listen to their expectations, as this part of it is more important than anything.

- I want you to coach me to get promotion at work

- I want you to coach me to learn to eat better food

- I want you to coach me to discipline myself to achievement

- I want you to coach me to be a millionaire

The point is that this is the number one important piece of information that you need in order to establish if you can live up to their expectations. If you can't make someone into a millionaire or teach them to use

69

methods to become one, then you should not offer that service. The reputation of life coaches depends upon honest assessment of their expectations and knowing that if they follow your methods, they can achieve their goal.

Be organized

When you only have a couple of clients, it is easier to track your schedule and the progress of each of your clients. But when you acquire more clients, it will become very hard for you to remember the particular issues that each client is dealing with and the corresponding status of their life coaching programs. This is why you need to keep an organized portfolio for each of your client where you can record all of their details. If you rely just on your head to remember things, you will soon miss client meetings and forget tasks that you need to finish for your clients. Eventually, you will end up with dissatisfied clients who can ruin your career in the long run. If you do keep a portfolio on each client, read it before the appointment. The client wants to feel that he/she is the most important person in your horizon at the time that they have their appointment. If you perpetually remind them of their insignificance by referring to their notes all the time, you are merely reinforcing that you don't know who they are and they are not important enough to you to have actually learned that. I put my papers away when I talk to clients. I want them to feel that they are the most important person in the room and to me, they are. It is sincerity that wins the day, rather than trying to beat the numbers game and having too many clients to actually give them their money's worth of coaching.

One of the benefits of being organized is that you will be able to give your full attention to your clients during your scheduled sessions. Your clients will feel that they are important to you and that you truly want to help them achieve their goals. They will appreciate that you remember to call when you told them that you would call or that you email them something that you promised to send them. You will not only be able to impress your clients but, more importantly, you will be able to earn their trust. Trust is huge in this business. If you don't return their calls or if you have to refer to your paperwork to catch what their first name is then you are in the wrong kind of business. In groups, perhaps this may be more acceptable, but when you are employed by a company to coach a group of people, the client isn't the employee. It's the company. In this case, as long as you give the company your full attention and professionalism, you are likely to continue to have your services requested in helping staff to develop new attitudes, goals and approaches.

Stick to a realistic schedule.

You will eventually discover what kind of schedule works best for you and your client. But a lot of life coaches claim that the optimal schedule for them is to meet each of their clients for about three times per month. There are certain clients who have bigger issues that may need more time with you. But others can work on their own and may need to meet with you for less than three times per month. You need to determine the amount of time you need to spend with your clients based on their individual requirements. If you deal with relationship coaching, and people seem particularly needy at the start of their dealings with you, you need to gear your program to meet those needs. In this, I mean that instead of letting yourself be too available for their emotional needs which may be overwhelming, get the client busy with different methods to reach set goals so that they don't have time to keep bothering you with emotional stuff that interrupts your other work. Basically, as a life coach you are going to be responsible for the time that your clients have with you. If you can set tasks for them to achieve between sessions, this helps to make them more accountable and takes a bit of the pressure off you.

You do not really need to always meet with your clients in person in order to hold your coaching sessions. Face to face coaching is definitely necessary at least a couple of times during the entire coaching program but there are instances when doing the coaching sessions over the telephone or via online tools such as Skype is effective enough. It is even a convenient option for your clients who are always out of town for business trips. Utilizing technology in your life coaching will enable you to reach more clients not only within your local area but also all over the world. When you do use worldwide techniques, these should include neuro linguistic approach because this is vital to understanding the needs of your clients and teaching them to deal with their goals in a much more open fashion.

Give more than just instructions

Do not think of yourself as a pricey advice giver. Being a life coach is more than that. You need to do more in helping your clients explore the different possibilities that are available to them. You need to help them determine which of those possibilities are best for them. You need to spend sufficient time with your client in order for them to modify the behaviors that are not helping them achieve their goals. When they talk to you, as I have stated before, listen to their answers to questions because this gives you a lot of information on the type of person that you are dealing with. This determines your approach because one approach for all is not an effective method of coaching. Your coaching needs to be niche orientated, so that you know you will get consistent results for that type of person by employing certain methods.

One effective way to fully involve your clients in the life-coaching program is giving them homework. This will enable them to put into action all lessons and techniques that you have discussed. The homework should involve positive actions that can help them execute positive changes in their lives. The whole purpose of homework assignments isn't really the same as schoolwork assignments. What the coach is looking for is positive results. They have the aim of the client in mind. They also know what needs to be done for the client to achieve a success level but it's important to develop a program that addresses those needs in little portions.

For example, a weight loss coach would discuss with the client his/ her weaknesses and teach that person to think in a different way so that the client does not feel deprived or go back to their old way of thinking. There should be set goals and these should start as relatively easy but get harder so that the client has to understand that the system being introduced is working in their favor. People don't want to be failures. People don't actually enjoy coming to a session telling a coach that they haven't done what they were asked to do. With the right enthusiasm from the coach and this is positive enthusiasm rather than criticism, the client should get results because that's what they are paying for.

CHAPTER 9

Develop Effective Coaching Skills

Show care and empathy

Most of the work that you will do as a life coach will involve assisting your clients in setting goals and motivating them to pursue those goals. You will be able to effectively do these tasks if you truly like being with other people in a pleasant and open manner. Your clients will find it difficult to confide with you their darkest fears and deepest desires if they sense that you are judgmental and self-righteous. You need to work towards gaining their trust because only when your clients fully trust you will you be able to effectively work with them in achieving their goals. Think of this on a very basic level. If you ask someone that you are close to if they can help you with a problem and you say that you can, they will expect that help until whatever the goal they are after is achieved. It's the same with coaching. If a coach teaches ineffective methods, the coach – having taken on the client – may have to adjust those methods in order to achieve the same results given the personality of the client will be a huge factor in whether they achieve or not. That's why the initial process of interview is so vital and should not be wasted with pleasantries. It's about finding out how someone ticks and speeding up the clock!

Show sincerity when helping your clients

It is not really expected that as a life coach, you will be nice and understanding 100% of the time. You are also human with your own personal issues and struggles. But as a life coach, you need to know that your clients will depend on you for moral support and motivation in achieving their goals. As such, you need to learn how to be sincerely supportive to your clients even when you are going through your own personal problems. Your life doesn't come into the picture, unless you have proven experience in your field that they respect. As far as your personality and private life are concerned, these should be kept out of the picture unless they are used to help the client. It's too easy to fail to see the difference between being someone's friend and being their life coach and this is where many people go wrong in the initial stages of being a professional. Yes, you are their confidante, but you are also being employed by them. It's unlikely you will ever become friends outside of the field of work that you are dealing with, so keep your "opinions" out of the picture.

It is also possible that one or two of your clients are really not the nicest people in the world. But since they are your clients, you need to be able to handle them despite the dislike that you feel for them. You need to learn how to look beyond people's flaws and imperfections so you will be able to help them achieve their highest potentials. There will be clients who appear to be receptive to your methods but who disappoint by not actually bothering to do the homework set. In cases such as this, they do need to be reminded that coaching requires work from both parties and that if this is not going to happen, you are not prepared to coach them any longer. It's not about you doing it for them. It's about them learning to do things for themselves.

Always keep in mind that your clients are not really your personal friends

You may be intimate with your clients' darkest fears and deepest desires but it doesn't mean that you are expected to become their personal friends. You are not expected to hang out with them or invite them to your personal affairs. Always remember that you are their coach and your primary responsibility is to motivate them and help them achieve their goals. You always need to keep in mind that your relationship with your clients is a professional one with certain limits or boundaries. You are not their fairy godmother though many unrealistic people expect you to be. Know when to say "no" and where to draw the line because otherwise clients will have you doing all the running and that is not what coaching is all about. You need them to stick to the plans that you draw out for them and to show progress at each step of the way, so that they can't say you didn't fulfill your promise. They need to make the actions, change the attitudes and try

76

out new techniques to get what they want from life and it's your place to show them those methods that they may not be familiar with that help them to achieve that.

Learn how to be flexible

Since you will be dealing with clients who are going through certain issues in their lives, it is quite common for you to experience getting a call from them at night or even during your rest days. As such, you need to be open to the possibility that your working hours will not be strictly 9 to 5. Some days may be easy because you only need to work with a client for an hour. Other days may be more hectic because you need to talk to more clients that you have planned for. You need to practice discernment in determining which issues are truly urgent and which issues can be put off until your next coaching session. The importance of setting tasks as part of the coaching process cannot be overemphasized. This keeps clients heading in the right direction, but the goals that you give them must be realistic so that they see positive results. Remember, a lot of people who ask for the help of a coach have little confidence. They may demand a lot at the beginning but your course should be written in such a way that they know what they have to do within a set timeframe and as they achieve the goals that you do set, they will start to feel a certain amount of self-satisfaction which will make them less dependent upon you and more dependent upon themselves to gain results. That's the whole point of coaching.

You also need to be flexible enough to revise the original coaching program for your clients if you see that they are not really giving you the results that you want to have. Some things may change along the way so you need to always keep an open mind to discern when it is appropriate to take another path in order to help your clients achieve their goals.

Unleash your creativity

More often than not, you will not be able to use the "recipe" advice that is readily available on the Internet to help your clients achieve their goals. Remember, you will be dealing with unique individuals with unique problems and goals. You need to unleash your creativity in thinking of strategies and techniques that will be most effective for your clients. You need to think out of the box. Sometimes, you may need to look at the problem from different perspectives in order to see the best solution. You owe it to your client to come up with a coaching program that will enable them to achieve their goals.

I can give you an example here. Classic coaching for people starting out in a new life after bereavement takes them through the standard process of grief. However, grief in itself is not standard. It is personalized to every person who has to deal with it. I have tried the creative approach with many clients by getting them to do tasks on their own that they have never done before. Perhaps the client depended too much upon their partner and have no idea how to move forward in their lives. Creative solutions included making them take driving lessons, opening a banking account and achieving things that they never thought themselves capable of. They came to me in a very vulnerable situation and gradually the coaching helps them to see that as an individual, the client is actually strong enough to do all of these things that they believe themselves incapable of. It works the same in any kind of coaching. You come up with creative tasks that fit in with the client's fears and get them over those fears.

The more creative and personalized you can make your services, the more people gain from them and at the end of the day, what you see is a whole person who now has what they were seeking in their lives. That's a very satisfying accomplishment. A sports coach who sees someone achieve something for the first time knows that the client has found that inner strength to achieve. Similarly a financial coach who sees a client being able to handle financial affairs in such a way that they are unquestionable will see the same sense of satisfaction from a client because they may not have thought of the approach that you are using, when educational systems and methods let them down.

Good Coaching Qualities

Unlike other businesses, like consultancy, advisory work, providing training or another professional type of service in which you complete work on the behalf of your client, coaching is different. Coaching is where you are working with your client and the qualities you need are also very different from those in the other jobs:

- **Listening** – Listening is a far more important quality than talking for a life coach. If you can listen, you can hear the things that are not said, the things that can help you to overcome whatever fears they have. It is what will help you to be completely objective and give them your undivided attention and support. Being a good listener leads to the next skill, the ability to ask the right questions at the right time. If you have a client who is afraid of failure, you need to program your course, so that they begin to see success and lose their fear of failure. You have to be adaptable to their needs and meet them. You have to back this up with pages on your webpage that give them reading that will help with the methods that you introduce, based upon what it is that they say to you. Your listening skills are the most important skills of all because often you find that even if someone is finding it hard to discuss their own shortcoming, you can read between the lines if you are an attentive listener.

- **Communication** - Communication is a two-way street and, as well as being able to listen, you have to be able to interpret what you hear and talk to your client in a way that knocks any preconceived ideas, barriers and negativity out of the way. Good communication skills enable a feeling of trust and understanding between you and your client and you must be able to communicate your meaning and feeling, not just empty words. One of the biggest things you must not do is have an agenda when you are communicating with your client and you must never judge or influence their words. You are talking with people who are anxious, stressed and have hopes and dreams that they want to achieve – they need to know that you understand that. Good communication skills allow you to help your client to find the answers they seek without actually telling them the answer. They need to discover the answers for themselves. You are coaching them to be able to do this, and it will help them in all different areas of their lives in the future, rather than being something that is only of limited value now.

- **Building rapport** – rapport with your clients is absolutely vital to your job. If you have a true desire to help others then you should have no problem with this, especially as your focus is entirely on your client. One thing that I found was helpful with this is that you need to make the client feel that he or she is the center of your universe during the sessions. Don't let interruptions happen or it will make them question your loyalty to them. Have you ever been in a doctor's surgery pouring out your fears about an illness and then had the telephone ring? The doctor's attention is drawn to the telephone and suddenly, you feel like your whole talk with the doctor has been put on hold. Don't do that to clients or you will fail to build a rapport. A rapport comes from giving them all of your attention.

- **Inspire and motivate** – two more core skills that a life coach needs. Again, this is usually borne of your deep desire to help other people and you will find it easy to inspire them and to motivate them to do what they need to do. The very fact that you are taking the time out to help them is sometimes motivation enough. When a client succeeds in a goal that you have set, celebrate it. Make it a stepping stone. The stepping stone system is one that works well with life coaching. Write down what the client is hoping to achieve. Make your plan work around these needs and your homework should be broken into small pieces that fulfill one of these needs at a time. When the client achieves one step in that process, celebrate it. Make the client feel good about it as you work your way to the next stepping stone. I tend to ask clients what they want from me. After the initial session with a client, I sit with them for a few moments while we work out exactly what it is that the client wants to achieve:

  ☐ I want to feel independent

  ☐ I want to be able to do things on my own

☐ I need to prove to my father that I am a capable human being

☐ I need to show my boss that I am fit for promotion

Each of these goals can then be split into creative sessions where the client feels that he/she is ticking the boxes and learning the things that are needed and expected of the life coach. That way, there can be no question that you are meeting the needs of the client. The client can see the chart that you have made and can also celebrate ticking the boxes as life skills are learned, so that at the end of the course, the client cannot question the life coach on value for money.

- **Flexible and Courageous**. Every life coach has a different pattern to the way they work. You cannot predict what will happen when a client comes to you for help so there is no set formula to follow. Keep in mind that each person is different and has very different needs and do make sure you take human emotion into account.

  What that essentially means is that life coaches have to take their lead from what they get back from the client. Thus, listening is vital, but learning what underlying wants the client has is what's even more vital because these form the stepping stones of learning that will enable the client to achieve everything that they want to achieve.

Coaching is also a client-led process, which means the emotions have to be tapped from your very first meeting. Being flexible enough to react to different circumstances and having the curiosity it takes to understand what is really going in with them is crucial. All of this takes courage and you must have a real strong belief in yourself and your abilities as well as the determination to do what is needed for your client.

After the client has told you what it is that they are looking for, that's the hard part done. However, be cautious in assuming what they want. That's why I always go over a plan of attack with the client and say to them after writing down what I see as their goals:

Would you look at this page of goals and tell me how accurate you think it is.

At this stage, a client may say that it isn't accurate and may want to discuss what's not accurate and what you have misread about their wants and needs. This gives you the opportunity to get those goals exact and when you have, print them out for you and the client and date the paper and sign it, getting the client to sign it as well. This means that you and the client are sealing a deal together to get them what they want. There can be no argument about what it is that you are supposed to help them with and instead of making this a safeguard for you, you use it as their reminder of what the goals are. People are very changeable and when they start saying that they want this or they want that and show dissatisfaction, you can reinforce that the goals you are working toward are those written on the contract and that these need reaching before any changes are made, except where these are related and can perhaps help in the achievement of the initial goals.

Principles of Coaching

All good coaches work by these principles:

- Listening is far more important than talking

- You must understand what motivates your client

- Believe that everyone is capable of more than they are doing

- You cannot base a person's future on their past. However, their past may help you to understand their motives better

- Each client has only one real limit – their belief in what they can or can't do. You need to keep that belief in them strong at all times.

- Life coaches must always provide a high level of support. You are there for the client and while they are paying you, need to be accountable.

- A life coach never gives the answers, only helps a client to find the answers for themselves. The discovery of an answer on the part of the client is so vital to their development so don't give answers. Let the work you do with the client and the consequent actions that they take provide them with answers.

- A life coach never criticizes anyone during the course of their work. This is degrading and does not help client/coach relationships. It can only add negativity.

- Everything discussed between you and your client is confidential. If you are taking on relationship and personal development clients, make sure that they know this as it may worry them.

- A life coach must be able to recognize those that cannot be helped by coaching and refer them to the right person. There may be cases that are beyond your help and this could be because the client has health problems or even psychiatric problems that are beyond the scope of your expertise. Do refer these cases to the professionals if you feel that they need it. You can do this by giving them the number of someone who can help, but you cannot discuss their case with these professionals outside the scope of your confidentiality agreement with your client. Perhaps the client will ask you if you can go with them and that's really down to your professionalism and is your own choice.

Who Can Be a Life Coach?

Life coaches can be anyone; they can come from any walk of life, any kind of background. A life coach would generally come from a profession where they have had contact with people, have helped other people and like to help and care for others, such as:

- Teaching

- Nursing

- Management

- Consulting

- Prison Service

- Therapy

- Counseling

- Training

- Complementary Therapies

- Human Resources

- Personal Trainers

- Voluntary workers

- Charity workers

- Armed forces

- Emergency services

- Service industries

How Does Becoming a Life Coach Help Me?

Apart from the financial side, becoming a life coach can help you to develop your own character, your humanity skills and can add a very rewarding new perspective to your life. A typical person who wants to become a life coach would be looking for a new direction in life, a deep willingness to learn new skills and a real passion for helping others. They will be a positive person with a positive outlook and will be qualified in different life coaching techniques.

Learning to become a coach generally involves a great deal of learning about yourself and most find that they have personal issues that perhaps weren't so apparent before they started. Issues must resolved before you can go on to coaching other people. Since you need to give your client 100 percent, you need to be 100 percent ready and able to do this.

Becoming a life coach is a very serious commitment and a big step. It will involve changing your life goals, setting new ones that go a long way beyond just learning something new and starting a new career. There are lots of different routes you can go down, lots of places you can go to get your certifications and accreditation, which is fast becoming formalized now across the world.

Learning to become a life coach doesn't necessarily mean that you have to start your own business either. Many large organizations look for life coaches or personal coaches as way of bringing a new perspective to their training and development solutions for employees, including the managers and executives.

The very nature of life coaching means that you are able to bring a very different and highly effective approach to the workplace, teaching positive behavior, developing integrity, mentoring skills, ethics, humanity, emotional maturity and culture, to name just a few. All of these are vital to the success of any organization and are a direction that you could very easily go in once your training is complete whether for a private company or for yourself.

Over the years, life coaching is something that has become recognized and is used by people in all kinds of situations. It isn't just the elite. It isn't just the rich. People are finding that their lives need that extra push toward success and that's where life coaching comes into its own. The methods that you learn help people to achieve. They are willing to pay for your expertise because they want to steer their lives in a certain direction. You help them to do that. It's not about your ideas. It's about helping others to develop their own ideas.

CHAPTER 10

The Seven Secrets of the Most Successful Life Coaches

Life coaching is a red-hot career right now and, with so many people jumping on the bandwagon, believing that they have what it takes to be a successful life coach, I thought I would share with you seven secrets to success in this career path. These secrets come from the top life coaches; people who have strived hard to get to where they are now and know just what it takes to do it.

It doesn't matter what you do for a living now, if you are looking to change careers, boost your income, and explore a new world, life coaching may seem like the obvious place to be. You see all these gurus all over the Internet making the big bucks and you believe that you can do it too. We've all seen the adverts, we've all heard the speeches but the biggest question is – what makes the top life coaches different from those who try and fail? And, are the any opportunities to be a life coach or is it a saturated career field where there's nothing left for anyone else? The key to your success lies in these seven secrets.

Secret Number 1 – Get Real

Forget the adverts that promise you can become an instant success overnight that you can soon be rolling in riches beyond your wildest dreams. Everywhere you look in the world of life coaching, extravagant promises litter the way. Some sites promise that all you really need is the "gift of the gab" while others say it is nothing more than painting by numbers.

People who are already in a career that requires contact with people, such as a social worker, may find promises of earning $200 for a brief session with a client almost too much to pass up on. The reality is most coaches don't earn that and many never will. In a recent study, it was found that 70% of life coaches don't even break the $50,000 per year mark and nearly 40% never made it to $10,000 per year. Only 10% of life coaches earn in excess of $100,000 per year and those are life coaches to highly successful Fortune 500 companies.

The same study determined that almost 100% of those questioned stick to one on one life coaching instead of the group telephone sessions that so many websites proclaim to be a real goldmine. While these figures have undoubtedly changed in the recent past, they do give an idea of the realities of becoming a life coach and the big picture shows that, like most people in business, it is only a small percentage who earn the big money. There are successful coaches and there are those who are broke and there are some who never get a result with a client and who really shouldn't be coaching anyway. They are there because someone told them they could earn a fortune and they trained and certified anyway regardless of their own ability and personality.

The implications of the studies are very clear. Life coaching is not a magic pill, it is not an overnight moneymaker and it certainly is not for everyone.

Secret Number 2 – Be Prepared to Commit 100% of Yourself to Life Coaching

The numbers of life coaches continues to grow year on year and those who are simply sitting back and watching are all asking the same questions – has supply completely outstripped demand and are there just too many life coaches in the same arena now? There is another group of people who believe that the real money is not in life coaching anymore. Instead, it is in coaching those who want to be a life coach.

Certainly, the consensus seems to be that, while there are certainly an awful lot of would-be life coaches jumping on the bandwagon, there are even more unsuccessful ones falling off it each year. Competition is still hard but the recent financial crisis has more than likely thinned out a lot of people who simply can't afford not to be in a steady job. One way of looking at it is that the large turnover in the business means that there is always opportunity for someone else to join in. Life coaching as a career is still relatively young and there is plenty of space but it takes true commitment to be successful and there will always be that demand for a successful coach.

Consider this – there are more than half a million psychiatrists across the US alone and only 30 - to 50,000 life coaches. Life coaching is a far easier prospect to sell than psychotherapy so life coaching is a growth market – a very big one. It is here to stay and is fast becoming an obsession but, at the same time, it is also a solid profession with the biggest growth being seen in large organizations and corporations hiring life coaches on a full time basis.

In order to succeed as a life coach, those who are newly certified have to devote 100% of their time to developing themselves and their business. They must be fully committed to succeed instead of just playing about at being a life coach. There are a lot of the latter types and sooner or later they come to the conclusion that they are not successful and that, just maybe, coaching isn't for them after all. But, if you have the passion to succeed then you have the passion to commit 100% to being a life coach. While you may face some stiff competition, there are plenty of resources on hand that at are designed to help you become successful.

So how does this fit with what was previously said in another chapter about not giving up your work for life coaching? The fact is that you need to pay your way and the advice given to people starting out on this career was not to put all their eggs in one basket until the business is secured and bound to provide a living wage. However, 100 per cent is expected on all life coaching work. Thus, if you spend two hours a day on life coaching, that two hours must be exclusive to life coaching and a period when 100 per cent of your effort is put into the task at hand. If you try this half-heartedly between coffee breaks with friends, it won't work. The devotion of your effort has to be 100 percent during your working hours and self-discipline is the biggest factor to take in when you are considering this as a career choice. If you cannot give 100 percent, you won't succeed.

Secret Number 3 – Make Sure Your Training is Top Notch and You Get the Right Credentials

The life coaching industry is maturing over time and, in order to succeed, coaches must have top-notch credentials to their names. Without them, there is no way of being able to sell themselves as experts in their field. The trick is to be bold but also to be prudent. Obviously, as a new life coach, you want to have your business up and running as soon as you possibly can, but many will fall at the first hurdle. This is simply because they have been sucked in by the flashy ads that promised high-speed training and these methods simply do not work. You cannot learn all you need to learn to gain accreditation in life coaching in a matter of days; it simply isn't possible. There aren't enough hours in the day for a start and there is just too much information to take in for a fast-track course to be of any use. The only winners are the people who are charging you good money to teach you a limited amount.

If you cut corners, you will pay the price - maybe not straight away but certainly somewhere down the line. Many of these so-called training courses charge in excess of $10,000, many asking for a sizeable deposit up front that is not refundable. They exaggerate how much you can earn and you have absolutely no hope of validating their claims.

Do your research before you sign up to any training course. Ask questions, interview them, look on the Internet and talk to other students. This is a large sum of money we are talking about and it's not an amount that anyone wants to waste. And, as of yet, the life coaching industry is not really regulated to the extent that other professions are, leaving it wide open to abuse. You cannot buy success.

Life coaching is reputable and anyone who joins it must be fully prepared, trained, have integrity and the ability to be professional with his or her clients. It takes a lot of time and effort to build up a business like this and if you are not fully prepared, it won't work.

Secret Number 4 – Think the Way an Entrepreneur Thinks

There is nothing like building up your skills and your confidence but if you truly want to succeed as a life coach, you have to get yourself from a training mode into the mode of building up your business. The one thing that stands out amongst those who try and fail to become successful life coaches is that they all spend too long focusing on their own personal development at the cost of mastering the skill sets needed to be a success. Because they have had a bad time of things, they quit the field and leave it, thinking that there is no way for anyone to become a life coach. What they don't seem to grasp is that anyone can become a life coach provided they buckle down and learn the critical skills, the core competencies needed to run a successful business.

In order to succeed, you must spend time sharpening your skills in business and never ever forget that this is what you are doing – building up a business, not playing a game where it's easy to make millions. You must be able to calculate your cash flow and come up with a top class but cost effective marketing plan, including social media as well as being able to help your clients succeed in their goals. You must take on the persona of an entrepreneur and have the fortitude and stamina of a marathon runner.

Secret Number 5 – Find the Right Niche

General life coaches will find their career a much harder uphill struggle than one who chooses a specific area in which to specialize. In ten years' time, a general life coach will still be struggling to earn more than $20,000 a year simply because they refuse to go into a specific niche.

Choose the niche area that suits you and research it from every angle you can think of. Look at whether people in that niche actually require life coaching. You are looking for a market that is hungry enough to snap your hand off, ready to pay whatever it takes and you need to be able to get to that market with ease. According to research, leadership and executive life coaches earn the most money but to get to a place where you can offer that you must have absolutely faultless business credentials.

The second highest earners are those who go into life coaching for small to medium businesses to help them improve their profitability, manage time better, set goals and reach them, etc. And in third place are skills life coaches, people who specialize n coaching sales teams on how to prepare better presentations, or help a company CEO to prepare for and manage a vital interview.

One other thing that has come from the research is that around 85% of life coaches started their working life within the business world, usually as consultants or human relations professionals. The remaining 15 % come from the mental health sector but, as the years pass and life coaching gains popularity, more and more people are coming from the social work sector.

Be aware that soft niches typically do not command such high earnings as others do but there is still plenty of competition. It is not very often that you find a narrow niche, one that has a small spectrum of clients. Social workers who have turned into life coaches can choose from any number of specialist niches, such as health, wellness, parenting, relationships, retirement and much more besides. Perhaps a social worker who has come from a background of caring for those with Alzheimer's can find a place in that niche while others may choose to go a little more diverse and look at weight issues, vocal performance, or perhaps providing help to those who are struggling with acting or becoming an artist of some kind.

A social worker who has a medical career background can find a home coaching emergency department physicians, cardiac surgeons, psychiatrists, even hospital administrators but they must be fully aware of the lifestyles, challenges and struggles of these particular professions, they must understand what makes them tick. A medical social worker could consider life coaching for professionals from any number of different disciplines as a way of managing stress, and balancing life and work.

In all honesty, as a life coach you can go as deep as you want or you can provide for very surface results. Whichever niche you choose to specialize in you must understand what their trigger points are.

Secret Number 6 – Building up your client base

Without clients, there is little point in you training to become a life coach so one of the most important things that you have to do is build up an effective marketing program. Being successful at life coaching means being able to solve problems and help other people but it also means you have to be able to promote yourself as well. No one else is going to send you any clients so you have to go out there and get them for yourself. It's up to you to identify and attract your client base to you and keep the coming, as well as referring others to you as well. There are lots of ways that you can self-promote, including:

Web site - having a well-designed high quality website is your starting point, a site that gives advice and answers questions as well as encouraging people to come to you. Perhaps consider offering the first session free or access to a free e-course. Remember the carrot is always important. Readers will want to know "What's in it for me?"

E-Newsletters – Build up an email list and send out helpful e-newsletters; make sure they are tailored to your audience and don't forget a call to action with an added incentive for potential clients.

Articles – Write articles in your niche, and get them published in magazines, trade papers, newspapers and on all the article submission directories. Make them relevant, up to date and interesting to read. Make sure you focus on problem solving and prompting new clients to contact you

Tele-seminars and Podcasts – These are always a good way, once you have a database of clients, to make the connection deeper by offering up a free teleseminar. An idea for this would be to turn one of your best articles into presentation that could be downloaded. Podcasts are a great presentation for potential clients so that they can see what your coaching is all about and establish if it's actually what they are looking for.

Go into Partnership with Other Business – Build up alliances with clubs or publications that already have a good database of clients. Be choosy about who you partner up with, certainly don't go mad and sign up with everyone. Use their lists to contact people and invite them to download a free e-course or a free teleseminar. Encourage them to join your website and sign up for your mailing list.

Don't go trolling for clients overtly but do use specialized message boards. Answer questions with authority, point people in the right direction for additional resources and clients will come running in their droves. At the end of the day, they are not buying life coaching; they are buying your expert services and solutions.

To get people to see that you are an expert in solving their problems, build up a platform that is visible, one that puts you head and shoulders above the competition. Make your website an exciting place to be, a place where you can link your visitors to your articles, newsletters, seminars and other educational material.

Lastly, use social media in a big way. Social media sites such as Facebook, LinkedIn and Twitter can vastly increase the number of people that visit your site and it costs nothing to do. In fact, used in the right way, social media marketing is the most powerful tool for you to use. Because they are social, by the time someone hires you, they already feel like they know you.

Secret Number 7 – Know and Understand What Success Means to You Personally

There is no definition of success in life and there are no benchmarks for success in life coaching. For a handful of life coaches, that success may be the publication of a number of books, writing a load of articles for high profile magazines, picking up thousands of followers on Twitter or appearing on two high profile shows in the same week or month. For others, it could be that they have made a real change, a real difference to the lives of 20 new clients each year.

If business does go through a slow patch, do not sink into the quagmire of believing that life coaching is not for you, of doubting your effectiveness as a life coach. Every business goes through these patches and it's up to you to pull yourself through it on the strength of your beliefs. I measure the level of my success by the number of people I am able to help to solve their own life problems.

Conclusion

Thank you again for buying this book!

I hope it was able to help you to better understand what it takes to become a successful and influential life coach. Although you need to go forward and learn all the methods that life coaches use, the book gives you all the information you need to consider before spending money on setting up a business that may not be fruitful. I cannot emphasize enough how important all this information is. It's not about you. It's about what YOU can offer your client. It's about putting all of your knowledge and education into enabling people to do what they want to do within the course of their lifetimes. Many avoid their wish list because they think it's too hard and too much of a struggle and live lives which are not satisfying as a result.

The methods that you learn when you take a life coaching course help you to impart all the knowledge clients' needs to put their lives into neat little boxes of achievement that don't restrict them or stop them from fulfilling their ambitions. You can help people to do that. You can help people to learn for themselves how it's done. You don't do it for them – but you enable them. It is this act of enablement that makes the difference between a teacher and a life coach.

When you experience the happiness of a satisfied customer, it's something that you won't forget in a hurry and that will fire you up with enthusiasm ready to meet your next client. Every satisfied customer is a testimonial to your abilities as a life coach, so never forget the opportunity to grab that testimonial while the iron is hot and place it onto your website and into your literature to help you keep developing your stream of clients for the future.

The next step is to use the lessons you have just learned in creating your own plans based on your area of interest, in order to become a great life coach that people respect and trust. Winning trust is everything –

positivity is everything – and attitude toward work will decide upon whether you succeed or fail.

Good luck!

Free Bonus Video: How to Be a Life Coach: Life Coaching Tips From a Successful Life Coach

This a great video on how to be a life coach with simple steps. Hopefully this helps on your journey to successfully helping people.

Bonus Video

https://www.youtube.com/watch?v=Qfb0D3ZdOP0

Made in the USA
San Bernardino, CA
24 September 2016